CREATIVE GARNISHING

CREATIVE

GARNISHING

····· BEAUTIFUL WAYS TO ENHANCE MEALS ·····

MARA REID ROGERS • PHOTOGRAPHY BY MICHAEL GRAND

A Running Press/Friedman Group Book

Running Press Book Publishers

Philadelphia, Pennsylvania

A RUNNING PRESS / FRIEDMAN GROUP BOOK

Copyright © 1991 by Michael Friedman Publishing Group, Inc.

9 8 7 6 5 4 3 2 1

Digit on the right indicates the number of this printing.

Library of Congress Cataloging-in-Publication Number 91-52575

CREATIVE GARNISHING:
Beautiful Ways to Enhance Meals
was prepared and produced by
Michael Friedman Publishing Group, Inc.
15 West 26th Street
New York, New York 10010

Editors: Sharyn Rosart and Elizabeth Viscott Sullivan
Art Director: Jeff Batzli
Designer: Marcena Mulford
Photography Editor: Christopher Bain

Typeset by Classic Type, Inc.
Color separations by Excel Graphic Arts Ltd.
Printed in Hong Kong by Leefung-Asco Printers, Ltd.

This book may be ordered from the Publisher.
Please include $2.50 for postage and handling.
But try your bookstore first!

Running Press Book Publishers
125 South Twenty-second Street
Philadelphia, Pennsylvania 19103

DEDICATION

....

*This book is dedicated to fellow food lovers around the world:
those who appreciate the natural beauty of food and love to eat!*

PART ONE
GARNISHING BASICS

PART TWO
GARNISHES

INTRODUCTION

To present your meals most enticingly, you might want to imagine that the plate is your canvas and the food your paint. The appearance of a plate of food is the source of first impressions which color our expectations of both the quality of the food and how it will taste. Not only should the food you serve taste wonderful, but it should be presented invitingly so that it tugs at the senses of taste, smell, and sight, while stimulating the appetite. Keep in mind that we do not eat for nourishment alone, but also for enjoyment.

Just as eating can be a source of pleasure, cooking and serving food can be a form of artistic expression. Superlative food presentation depends on several basic considerations. The use of fresh ingredients and good cooking techniques are of primary importance. One must also take into account the interaction of the food with the environment—how will the style, color, and material of the plate, napkin, and table setting affect the appearance of the food? The success of the presentation will be determined by how much attention you pay to each of these factors, plus the balance or harmony of all the elements as a whole.

One of the most influential aspects of the visual appeal of a plate of food is the garnish. The word garnish comes from the French word meaning "to adorn or furnish." In classical French cooking, garnishes, or *garnitures,* are side dishes. The term has the same meaning as our *accompaniments,* that is, any food presented in addition to the main item. In English the word *garnish* means to decorate a food by the addition of other items. The word is also used to signify these adornments.

There are several international influences that have affected Western garnishing practices. The first is the large vocabulary of classical French terms for specific garnishes. Though many of them have been changed slightly over time, their basic meanings remain the same, and the terms are well known to chefs. A word in the title of a dish can indicate either a single-food *garniture* or a *garniture* made up of a combination of foods. For instance, *crécy* refers to the addition of carrots, while *financière* implies the addition of many foods, such as veal quenelles, cockscomb, kidneys, mushrooms, shredded truffles, olives, and crayfish. The second garnishing influence that has inspired Western chefs is *mukimono*, the Japanese art of carving fruits and vegetables. Many garnishes used in *nouvelle cuisine* have evolved from this discipline.

Garnishing food is not strictly the province of professional chefs; it is an art for anyone who enjoys cooking and presenting good food. It need not be difficult or time-consuming; indeed, CREATIVE GARNISHING shows how the presentation of food can be simple, in good taste, and eye-catching.

CREATIVE GARNISHING presents neither the superfluous "apple swan" nor the outdated sprig of parsley, but imaginative garnishes that are not only simple to make but practical and effective. Also included are many garnishing tips and presentation ideas for meat, poultry, fish, vegetables, and salads, as well as fruit, desserts, and cheese. You may wish to follow the step-by-step garnishing ideas presented, or you may wish to let the book inspire you to create your own garnishes! When creating the garnishes in this book, be sure to read through the instructions completely before you begin a project, so that you'll have all the materials you need on hand.

If you are feeling creative, read the section on basic garnishing rules, then start looking at the sights around you for ideas. A successful garnish is based on the inherent beauty of food itself. It is never contrived or overworked. Just as a musician may find rhythm in the repetitive patterns of a flower or the light-reflecting scales of a fish inspire a potter's glaze, so may the designs, colors, and compositions found in nature inspire your garnishes. So, start playing with your food and, by all means, experiment.

Once you start garnishing, you will never again be satisfied with just an ordinary plate of food.

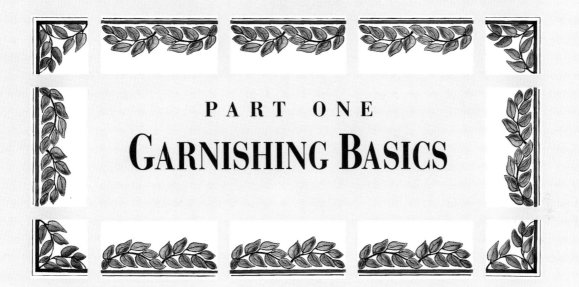

PART ONE
GARNISHING BASICS

CHAPTER ONE

THE TWELVE MOST IMPORTANT RULES OF FOOD PRESENTATION AND GARNISHING

• WATCH THE BALANCE •

• CHOOSE COLORS CAREFULLY • WATCH YOUR SHAPE •

• AT LEAST TWO TEXTURES TO A PLATE •

• FLAVOR WITH FINESSE • FLAVOR WITH CARE •

• MATCH THE AMBIENCE • SIZE UP YOUR SUBJECT •

• PLAN YOUR ARRANGEMENT • WATCH THE TEMPERATURE •

• SERVE ONLY EDIBLES • ALWAYS BE FRESH •

A garnish provides an enhancing visual element that gives a plate of food a special, finishing touch. It adds harmony to the organization of food on a serving dish. Naturally, a garnish cannot make a poor presentation beautiful, but it can make a good one great. A well-designed garnish can provide a focal point to direct the diner's gaze and unify a composition, whether the food is arranged on a plate, a platter, or in a bowl.

Though most presentations need to be garnished, some do not; if the accompanying vegetables, sauce, or other foods provide the interest, balance, and color that is needed, adding another element will confuse the presentation, rather than complement it.

When planning a garnish, take into account the mood and style of the main ingredient you are garnishing and the function of the garnish on that plate. Are you using the garnish to give height to a dish, such as Chinese Noodle Cages (see page 90), placed over sea scallops, or are you floating Sun-Dried Tomato Bridge Cuts (see page 44) in a bowl of clear consommé to add color? Whatever your intent, make sure that the final product is harmonious, not discordant. Always keep it simple, and let the beauty of the food speak for itself. Be sure to take advantage of the natural features of the ingredients you use, such as the unusual shape of a vegetable, the specific color of a fruit, or the texture of a grain.

The following "rules" will guide you to selecting the right garnish and using it in the most appropriate way every time.

1.   Watch the Balance Use foods and garnishes that give variety and contrast to your presentation, but be sure to avoid an overblown effect with too much contrast—it will be jarring. Balance is achieved through careful arrangement of color, shape, texture, flavor, and portion size.

DON'T   **DO**

2.   Choose Colors Carefully Imagine this plate: fillet of halibut topped with a cream sauce, white rice, and cauliflower. Boring. A plate of food all the same color is visually monotonous, and does not stimulate the appetite. The solution: Replace the white rice with wild, add some brussels sprouts instead of the cauliflower, and add a garnish. A garnish will quickly and effectively add an accent of color to brighten up your presentation and bring liveliness and interest to food arrangement. Be careful, however, to use a combination of foods whose colors harmonize. Just as an arrangement of too-similar colors will not whet the appetite, so a riotous arrangement of clashing colors will detract from the foods' appeal. If you find color decisions difficult, just brush up on the principles of the color wheel. Also do not forget your plate, platter, or bowl—there are many choices of colors in tableware that can add punch to your color scheme.

3. Watch Your Shape Just as important as attention to color is consideration of shape and forms. Do not plan a menu that includes all the same-shaped ingredients—diversity is critical. For example, while a plate of meatballs, peas, and pearl onions contains items that are too similar in shape to be interesting, a dish of meatballs with baby carrots and mashed potatoes is more visually exciting. The same consideration applies to garnishes: If you are serving a round food as a subject, do not repeat the shape with the garnish or it will look foolish. For example, peas should not be topped with a round garnish, such as Flower Blossom Butter (page 74), but would work well with an item of a different shape, such as the baby carrots.

DON'T   **DO**

4. At Least Two Textures to a Plate Texture of food is very important in terms of taste as well as appearance. Not only is a variety of color, shape, and form important to balance your presentation, but you must also have textural distinctions. Contrast the consistency of food and garnish. Do not make the mistake of serving too many soft or puréed foods. For instance, a plate of seafood mousse garnished with a pattern of tomato aspic, puréed asparagus, and a roll contains too many similar textures. If the mousse were garnished with a sprig of fresh dill, the asparagus left in spear form, and new potatoes substituted for the roll, the group of textures would be much more dynamic.

5. Flavor with Finesse

Flavor is not a visual element in food presentation; nevertheless, it is a direct influence. The flavor and style of the garnish should complement the meal. For example, an open-faced tofu burger with a side dish of bean sprouts has a health food aura, and requires a garnish that suits the food in flavor and style, such as Chive Braids (see page 67). Similarly, the character of the garnish should be appropriate to the type of food. For example, do not use a parsley sprig to garnish a dessert; use a mint leaf instead. If you follow this rule when using a more unusual ingredient for a garnish, such as an edible flower, the guest may not know what flavor to expect, but if it is compatible with the food garnished, such as a salad or dessert, it will be a perfect match and a wonderful surprise. The guest may still say, "What is a flower doing in my salad?" but he or she will then add, "This is delicious."

6. Flavor with Care

The flavor of the garnish should not come as a shock or be a bad surprise. Although a garnish should never be bland, the opposite is also true. So if you are using something flavorful, make sure it is not *too* flavorful or it will overwhelm the food—or the guests. For instance, do not garnish chili with whole jalapeños; even though the style of the garnish is appropriate, its flavor is not.

DON'T   **DO**

7. Match the Ambience When selecting a garnish, remember that the "flavor" or atmosphere of the room is an important factor. Just as the ingredients used to adorn food should match, so should the ambience of the room. Table settings and lighting can accessorize your food, so use them! Do not use a Mexican plate for a pasta course, but an Italian plate, nor serve delicate dessert such as petits fours in a room lighted by fluorescent lights. Likewise, be wary of using too little light. My sister-in-law taught me a great rule of thumb: one candle per person. So, while a romantic dinner for two can be lighted by two candles, a formal dinner for four should have four candles.

DON'T

DO

DON'T   **DO**

. . . .

8. Size Up Your Subject Coordinate the food you are serving with the size of the plate, platter, or bowl. A plate that is too small will make the food look awkward, oversized, and overcrowded—too large a plate, and the portions will appear meager. The main item (usually meat, poultry, or fish) is the subject of the presentation, and its portion should be slightly larger than the accompaniments so that it is the focus of attention. When there is no obvious subject, as in the case of a salad, form an appealing balance: Fan out the green lettuce leaves and other ingredients in an attractive arrangement, such as a "bull's-eye" pattern, then sprinkle red radishes julienne in the center. The same treatment applies to garnishes.

Strive for a garnish that is of the proper scale in relation to the other food items. A large grouping of vegetable slices would not be in keeping with a single, small medaillon of beef. Too small a garnish looks odd as well; imagine a single, small marzipan flower on a whole layer cake. Instead, try a cluster of marzipan flowers in the center or a ring of flowers around the edge of the cake. Also, do not over-sauce foods. It is a mistake to spoon so much brown sauce on top of a steak that it obscures the meat and how it is cooked. Use less sauce, and try ladling it around or under food.

Finally, consider height and weight. A flat, spreading garnish will make a beef medaillon appear smaller, whereas a small group of deep-fried beets carefully and neatly arranged in a loose pile in the center of the top of the medaillon will give it the illusion of height. If the food is delicate, a garnish that is cumbersome will not complement the food, and vice versa: A feather-light garnish does not enhance a dense type of food.

9. Plan Your Arrangement

9. Plan Your Arrangement The arrangement of food and garnish on a plate, platter, or bowl should be viewed as a whole. The food should not be stuck randomly and without thought, with the garnish placed wherever there is room left over. Instead, before you begin, decide how to arrange the food and where to place the garnish. When you are arranging the food on the dish, keep some space between items rather than grouping them in a mixed heap; it will help if you have chosen the correct plate size in relation to the food. Determine a focal point, and arrange the rest of the food so that the diners' eyes are manipulated, rather than pulled off to the edge of the plate.

Always display the best side of the food forward, and have the less attractive part of the food, such as the line of fat in a steak, face away from the guest. Be creative, and remember that the garnish does not always have to go on top of or next to food; it can also echo the border or rim of a plate.

DON'T   **DO**

10. Watch the Temperature Watch your temperatures. Always serve hot foods on a hot plate, and cold foods on a cold plate. Choose your garnish with respect to the temperature of the food to be adorned. For example, a garnish that has the potential to melt should not be placed on a hot food, unless melting is desired, as with a compound butter. Be organized and prepared, and plan ahead. You do not want to be fussing with last-minute details of a garnish on a hot plate of food, or it will be cold by the time you are ready.

•••

11. **Serve Only Edibles** Only ingredients that are edible should be presented with food, though sometimes toothpicks or skewers are needed to secure or hold together garnishes. Also, be very careful when using edible flowers and leaves: Always consult more than one professional authority or source—such as a book—before serving them or letting them touch food to be eaten.

•••

12. **Always Be Fresh** Garnishes should not be used to hide imperfections in food, such as bruises in fruit, or flaws in the table setting, such as a chipped plate because the garnish will draw even more attention to the original problem. Always use the freshest ingredients for your meals. Similarly, use garnishing ingredients that are as picture perfect as possible. Maintain their freshness throughout service, since usually they are the first item guests notice on a plate. Do not try to get away with using canned or frozen products for garnishes. Though these products are great for certain types of cookery as substitutions for fresh ingredients, they are not suitable substitutes for garnishes!

DON'T   **DO**

CHAPTER TWO

GARNISHING TOOLS AND TECHNIQUES

TOOLS: ESSENTIALS

• KNIVES • CITRUS ZESTER • GROOVED CITRUS CUTTER •

• VEGETABLE PEELER • MELON-BALL CUTTER •

• CORER • SCISSORS • TOOTHPICKS •

• TAPE MEASURE, RULER, AND PROTRACTOR •

• COOKIE CUTTERS • DEEP-FRYING TOOLS •

• PASTRY BRUSHES • ICE-CREAM SCOOPS •

• FOOD COLORING • WEDGE KNIFE •

• PARCHMENT PAPER AND DOILIES •

• ASPIC CUTTERS • SKEWERS •

TOOLS: NICE-TO-HAVES

• FLUTING KNIFE • BUTTER CURLER • MANDOLINE •

• TWEEZERS • FLUTED PASTRY WHEEL •

• PASTRY BAG • MOLDS • PASTA MACHINE •

GARNISHING TECHNIQUES

• STORAGE • PREVENTING DISCOLORATION •

• MAKING A STENCIL OR TEMPLATE • DISPLAY •

• BLANCHING AND REFRESHING •

TOOLS

Most of the tools needed for the garnishes in this book are fundamental utensils already in your kitchen drawer. This chapter divides tools into Essentials and Nice-To-Haves. If you do not already own a majority of these implements, they are very worthwhile investments toward a well-equipped and efficient kitchen. Tools from the Essentials list are common utensils that make a job easier. Tools from the Nice-To-Haves list include more unusual tools that allow you to try a technique or achieve an effect that could not be accomplished otherwise. It is true that you do not have to have an arsenal of gadgets, though it is easy (and fun) to be seduced by the vast array of kitchen equipment available. If you have a difficult time finding the more unusual tools in your area, please refer to the appendix (page 122) for resources to find kitchen equipment.

My favorite tool is a very specialized item—my treasured olive pitter. To me, it has become indispensable, though I have to admit it is not a necessity. Nevertheless, I find kitchen tools can provide inspiration for new ideas and offer many unexplored garnishing possibilities. Do try to expand your kitchen drawers and your garnishing repertoire.

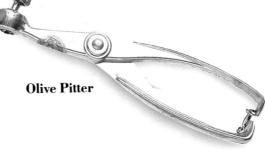

Olive Pitter

Knives

If you have only two tools to make garnishes, one of them should be a paring knife and the other a cutting board. A paring knife with a blade range from 2¼ to 4 inches (5 to 10 cm) long is a very versatile, all-purpose knife for making garnishes. Other knives that belong in your knife rack include a chef's knife (or French knife) with a blade that ranges from 8 to 13 inches (20 to 33 cm) in length, used for general cutting, and a serrated knife for slicing bread. Though there is a smaller version of a serrated knife made just for slicing tomatoes (called a tomato knife), any serrated knife will do double duty and is a very useful tool.

To get optimal use from your knives, they must be kept sharp. A sharpening stone or a professional knife-sharpening machine and a steel are required. I prefer to use a sharpening stone; it does not wear away the knife as an electric machine can, and it makes a better edge. A steel is a mandatory part of any knife kit. The steel is not used to sharpen the knife, but to "true the edge" (to smooth out irregularities) and to "maintain the edge" (to keep it sharp as it is used). Make it a habit to sharpen your knives and then fine-tune the blades with a steel afterward.

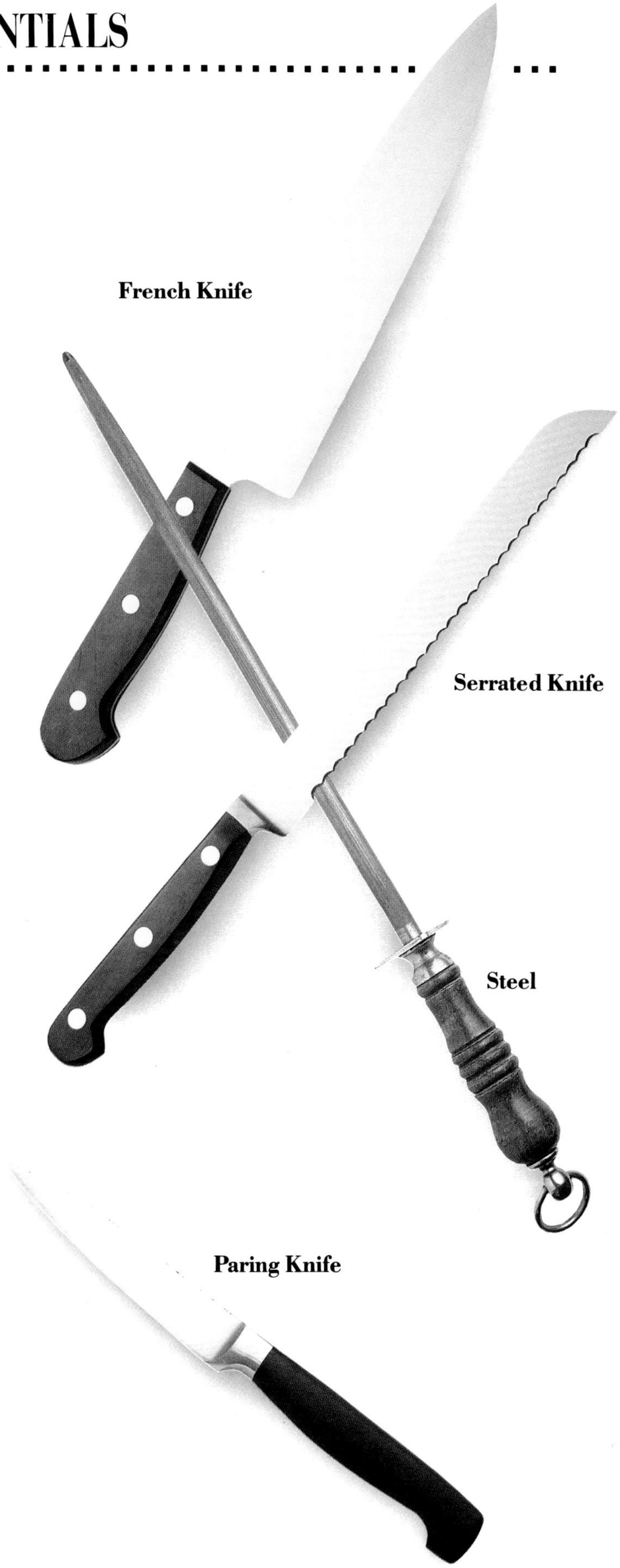

French Knife

Serrated Knife

Steel

Paring Knife

Citrus Zester

A citrus zester strips very thin slivers from the zest (outer skin, above the spongy white pith) of citrus fruits. This tool can be used for other fruits as well and to make designs in the skin of vegetables. If you score a grooved pattern into the skin of a vegetable and then cut it into slices, the result will be an interesting "striped" skin. Or use the zester to cut threads of skin from vegetables such as carrots and zucchini.

   To use a citrus zester, hold the bent end angled down against the food, and pull the zester into the food and along the surface of the skin, applying even pressure. Delicate threads of skin will form and push through the row of holes in the zester.

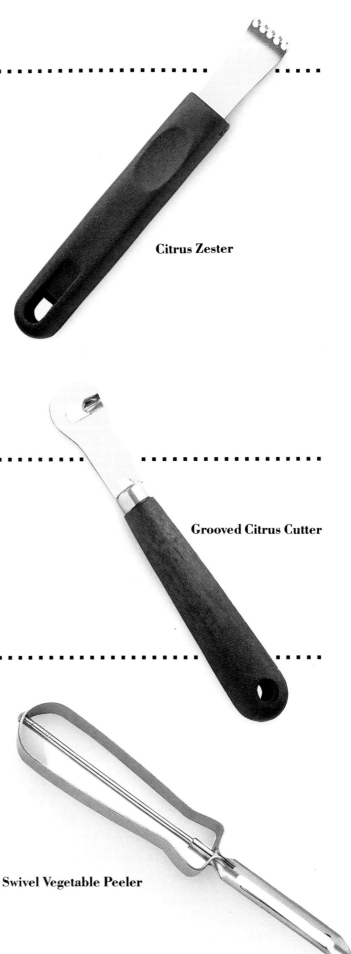

Citrus Zester

Grooved Citrus Cutter

Swivel Vegetable Peeler

Grooved Citrus Cutter

A grooved citrus cutter performs the same basic functions as a zester, but it cuts a single strip of skin at a time, and it goes into the white pith, not just the zest. It will cut a strip $\frac{1}{4}$ inch (6 mm) wide and $\frac{1}{8}$ inch (3 mm) deep. It is also known as a citrus stripper or channel knife.

Vegetable Peeler

I recommend using a swivel vegetable peeler, because this type does not cut too deeply into the food. It requires periodic sharpening, but for the minor cost and convenience, you may simply wish to purchase a new one each year.

Melon-Ball Cutter

Melon-ball cutters are available in a range of sizes and types. They are even available in fluted and oval shapes. If you only own one, make sure it is the plain, standard-size cutter, which is round and about 1 inch (2.5 cm) in diameter.

This tool can make round balls from the flesh of fruits and vegetables. To use it, start by cutting deeply into the fruit, rotate the tool, and then finish rotating until you come all the way around again, to cut a complete ball. Then use the edge of the cutter to cut and release the ball from the fruit or vegetable.

Melon-Ball Cutter

Corer

Though a corer is sometimes referred to as an apple corer, it is a marvelous tool for removing the core from almost any fruit, including tomatoes and pears. A corer removes the core perfectly in one swipe and leaves behind a clean-cut, even tunnel.

Corer

Scissors

I like to keep on hand a pair of small, sturdy, scissors with fine points for working with food and larger scissors for cutting paper. The smaller scissors can snip fresh herbs, trim the edges of pie crusts, and cut garnishes that are too difficult to cut with a kitchen knife, such as circular or triangular pieces of food. The larger scissors are great for opening boxes and packages of food and cutting out stencils from parchment paper and templates from cardboard or a heavy-stock paper. Scissors belong in your kitchen drawer—just make sure that they do not mysteriously relocate to someone's desk or to the tool shed!

Scissors

Toothpicks

Just as people come in different shapes, so do toothpicks! There are flat wooden toothpicks and round wooden toothpicks. I prefer round, only because they do not splinter as much when you break them, if, for example, you only need a short piece to fasten a garnish. Toothpicks are perfect for fastening and securing certain garnishes. They should be concealed, and any excess length trimmed off. They can also be used for skewering foods if you want a smaller presentation than is possible using the longer, standard skewers.

Round Wooden Toothpicks

Tape Measure, Ruler, and Protractor

I like to have on hand a small tape measure in addition to a ruler, not only because it is so compact, but because you can bend it if necessary, such as when working with pastry. A ruler is a necessity for making a straight edge, and is useful when working with garnishes that can demand exact measurements. A protractor is helpful, but for the garnishes in this book, any angles required are basic and are just as easy to figure out with the edge of a ruler.

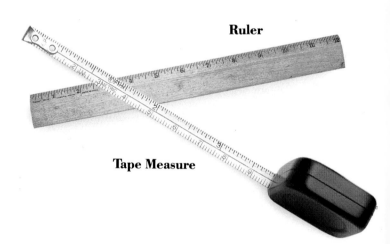

Ruler

Tape Measure

Cookie Cutters

If you are not an avid cookie-cutter collector already, start your garnishing collection with a round cookie cutter, a diamond-shaped cutter (which you can use also to cut triangles), a heart-shaped cutter, and a star-shaped cutter. A set of concentric-circle cutters, ranging from 1 to 4 inches (2.5 to 10 cm) in diameter can be very useful. These are available both plain and with fluted edges. Do not try to economize by using a drinking glass instead of a cookie cutter—the glass will break and the food will be studded with shattered glass.

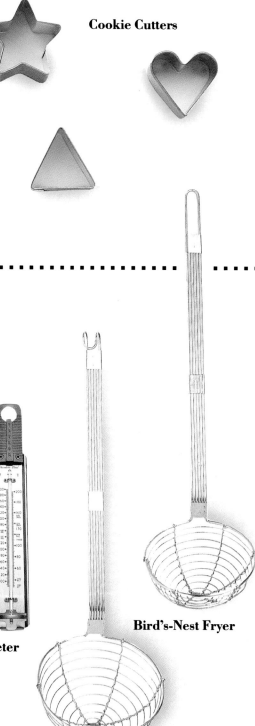

Cookie Cutters

Deep-Frying Tools

A candy-jelly-deep-fry thermometer is a tool that makes judging the stages of cooking sugar or heating fat easy. You can waste a lot of food trying to judge the temperature of sugar or fat without a thermometer. This is an indispensable tool when frying or making garnishes of sugar.

Other indispensable utensils for deep-frying are professional, long, flameproof oven mitts and a pair of metal tongs with long handles. For more unusual garnishes, such as Chinese Noodle Cages (see page 90), a bird's-nest fryer is needed. Available in several sizes, it is composed of two wire baskets that sandwich together to hold foods being deep-fried into the shape of "nests."

Candy-Jelly-Deep-Fry Thermometer

Bird's-Nest Fryer

Pastry Brushes

Pastry brushes are available in many sizes. Use them for decorating pastry and painting sauces. They are also good when used perfectly dry to decorate food with ground spices, herbs, and edible silver and gold dust. Keep separate brushes for specific uses—don't use a meat-basting brush for pie crust! Here's a very ingenious idea: a "pastry drawer." My father-in-law keeps all his pastry gadgets in one drawer, ever since he found one of his children using it to brush the dog.

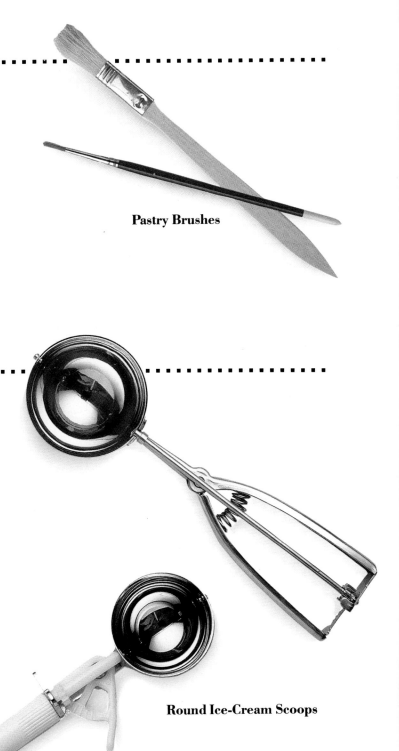

Pastry Brushes

Ice-Cream Scoops

Ice-cream scoops are available in three shapes: round, oval, and conical (the latter may be difficult to find), and they come in various sizes. In addition to scooping ice cream or sorbet, you can use a scoop to serve rice or other grains; to dish up salads, such as chicken and seafood; to serve potatoes; or even to form meatballs!

Round Ice-Cream Scoops

Food Coloring

I prefer to use vegetables such as onion skins or beets for coloring foods or sauces than to work with sets of dyes found at the supermarket. There are also baking stores where you can purchase professional bakers' dyes, which are referred to as "pastes" and come in a rainbow of colors. Do keep a set of food-coloring pastes on hand, however, because they are indispensable for coloring frostings and glazes, unless you want a beet-flavored frosting.

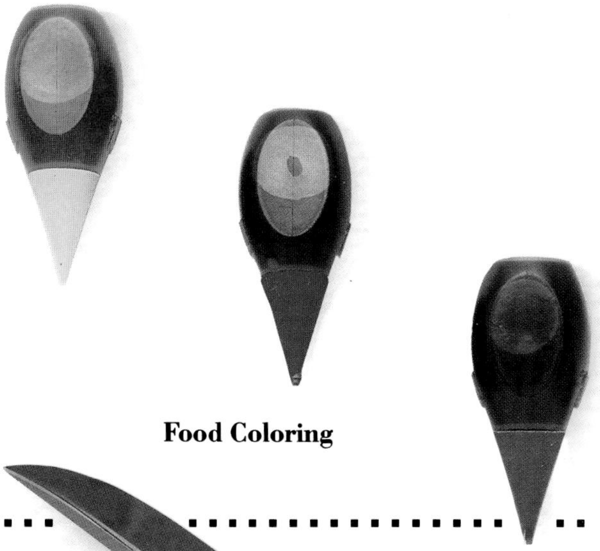

Food Coloring

Wedge Knife

A wedge knife creates uniform zigzag edges on melons, such as cantaloupe, honeydew, and watermelon. Using a wedge knife, cut a melon in half. Separate the halves, scoop out the fruit, and then use the shell for an attractive container for a fruit salad. Try this with other fruits and vegetables too!

Wedge Knife

Parchment Paper and Doilies

In addition to lining cake pans, parchment paper is great for making stencils. Doilies work well as ready-made stencils.

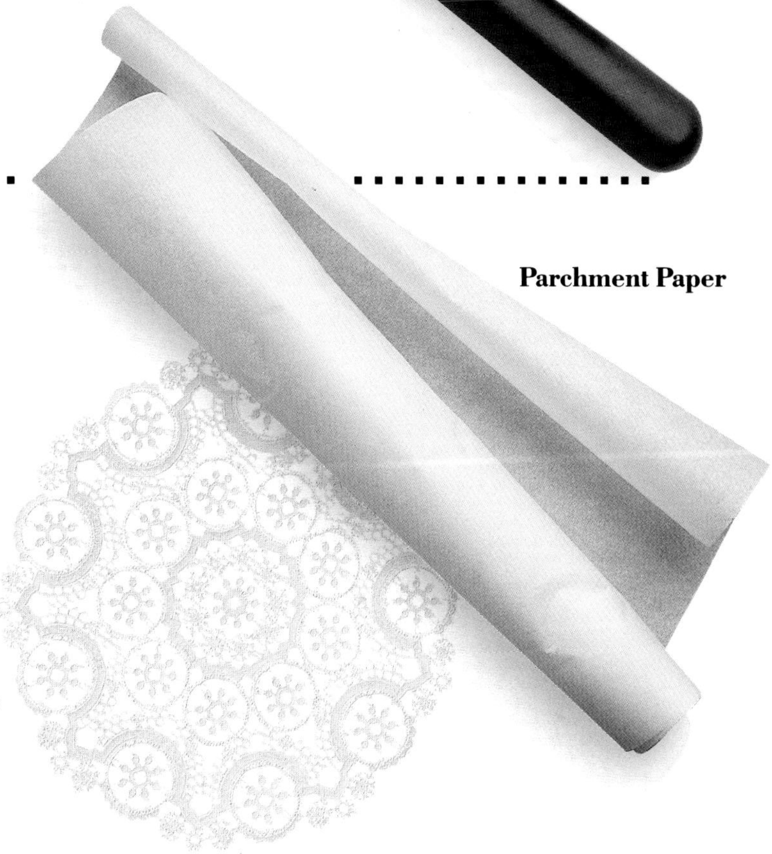

Parchment Paper

Doilies

Aspic Cutters

Though these can be more expensive than cookie cutters, they can broaden your decorating possibilities. Buy a small set of aspic cutters, which some call a "bridge set," because they illustrate the symbols from a set of playing cards—hearts, diamonds, clubs, and spades. These cutters can be very fun to use. Try using them to cut smaller foods, such as pimiento, hard-cooked egg whites, and pitted olives. They are also called truffle cutters.

Aspic Cutters

Skewers

Skewers are available in bamboo and metal. I use bamboo for shish kebab and other presentations that require skewering foods not only because they are more authentic, but they also do not impart a metallic taste, as some metal skewers do. However, the metal skewers are the only type that can be used to make "grill marks" as described in this book.

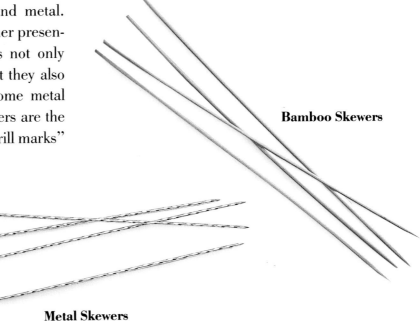

Bamboo Skewers

Metal Skewers

Fluting Knife

A fluting knife, also known as a corrugated cutter, is a specialized knife with a ridged blade. It cuts vegetables and fruits into slices resembling corrugated cardboard. This utensil works best with vegetables and fruits that have firm flesh, such as carrots, beets, turnips, and apples.

Three-Sided Fluting Knife

Butter Curler

Butter is a fun material for garnishes, and this implement is the quickest way to make a simple butter garnish. You may be trying not to eat a lot of butter, but that does not mean you can't play with it! The blade of a butter curler is shaped like a flat hook, and it has fine teeth on one side.

To use it, just cut into the butter, about 1/8 inch (3 mm) deep. Hold the cutter at a slight angle, and pull it toward you slowly, tooth side down, applying even pressure along the surface of a smooth, flat-sided stick or slab of butter. The hook will gradually form a "curl" of butter.

Butter Curler

Mandoline

A mandoline is more expensive than most non-electric kitchen tools, but it is one of the few utensils that truly is multipurpose, and it fulfills each function perfectly. It is mainly a slicing tool that can make different thicknesses of slices, weaves, crinkle cuts, and julienne strips of firm vegetables, such as potatoes and carrots. I find it makes more exact and uniform shapes than a food processor. Though you can substitute a box grater, it only does a few of the cuts the mandoline does. A mandoline also shreds well and is less time-consuming for most people to use than a knife.

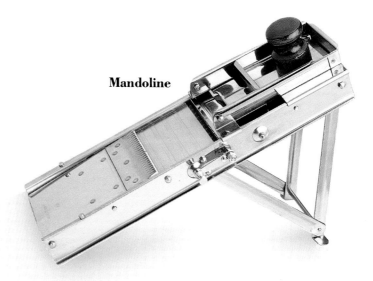

Mandoline

Tweezers

Tweezers can be very useful for moving food from one area to another, especially in hard-to-reach, tight places. Tweezers are available in a variety of styles; I prefer the longer, thinner variety.

Tweezers

Fluted Pastry Wheel

A fluted pastry wheel makes a zigzag edge on pastry or pasta, and is a perfect tool for cutting and sealing homemade ravioli.

Fluted Pastry Wheel

Pastry Bag

The pastry bag has many diverse uses. In addition to piping frostings for cakes and filling eclairs with cream, use it to draw sauces and melted chocolate onto plates or to make other garnishes. Try using a pastry bag to pipe mashed potatoes for the top of your favorite shepherd's pie recipe. There is a great assortment of styles and sizes of tips to use with the bag, from straight lines to leaves.

Pastry Bag

Molds

There are many types, sizes, and shapes of molds. These can be made from a wide variety of materials, including copper and plastic, depending on the mold's function. There are molds for butter, chocolate, custard, gelatin, ice cream, and more. Shapes range from ring molds to very realistic animal molds.

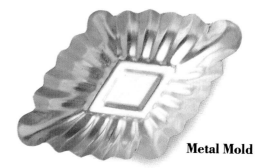

Metal Mold

Pasta Machine

I prefer a manual pasta machine over an electric one because an electric pasta machine tends to "cook" the dough. You may also roll your pasta dough with a rolling pin and cut it free-hand with a knife instead of using a machine, but be prepared to work very quickly or the dough will dry out before you've had a chance to finish cutting it.

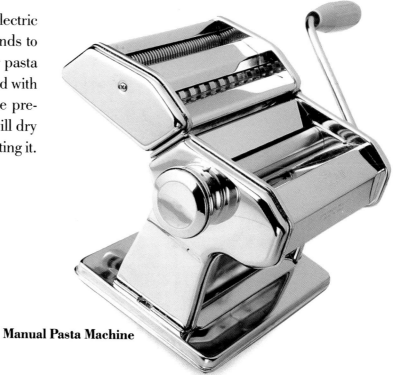

Manual Pasta Machine

GARNISHING TECHNIQUES

Each garnish project supplies you with all the necessary information you need, but here are a few hints you may find helpful, especially if you are creating your own garnishes.

Storage It's best to make garnishes just before serving, but if you need to make your garnishes beforehand, the best choices are any of the carved vegetable garnishes, which you'll find in Chapter Three, The Vegetable Garden. Although many of the other garnishes in this book can also be made ahead of time, in general, garnishes from Chapter Four, The Herb and Spice Rack, Chapter Five, The Bouquet, Chapter Six, The Exotic, and Chapter Seven, The Sweet Shop are made from foods that tend to be more perishable. When garnishes are made from more perishable ingredients such as caviar, caramel, and chocolate, they should be made as close as possible to the time of serving. When in doubt, use your judgment. Store garnishes as you would their components. If your garnish is made from a dried food, don't refrigerate it, just wrap and store it at room temperature. If it is made with ingredients that are usually refrigerated, then make an airtight seal by wrapping it in plastic wrap, and refrigerate until needed. (Always store the garnish in its own section of the refrigerator, where it won't get crushed by other foods.) Or, if it is made from only vegetables, cover the garnish in cold water until you are ready to serve it. Blot lightly before serving. Remember, you can always prepare the different parts of a garnish ahead of time and assemble it at the last minute.

Preventing Discoloration Some foods, especially certain fruits (such as pears, apples, bananas, and avocados) and vegetables (including mushrooms, potatoes, eggplant, and artichokes) will discolor quickly once cut. Close to the time of service, check the garnish to see that it looks fresh and its color is vivid. To slow down this discoloration process (although nothing will prevent it), soak the cut fruit in "acidulated water," a mixture of water and fresh lemon juice. A ratio of 1-1½ table-spoons (15-22 ml) for every 2 cups (.48 l) water works well.

Making a Stencil or Template Be sure to differentiate between stencil patterns and template patterns and follow the appropriate instructions. For a stencil, use the pattern as a guide and trace the design onto parchment paper. Cut out the design with scissors. The design should be clearly defined, with no torn or ragged edges. Pay particular attention to the center of the pattern, where it can be difficult to cut cleanly. Proceed with directions.

For a template, used in place of a cookie cutter to create designs, follow the stencil directions, but trace the design onto a transparent paper, such as onionskin, and then tape that over a piece of cardboard. Using a utility knife or other art blade in a safety holder, cut through the typing paper and the cardboard, following the design on the template.

If the food to be decorated is firm and/or dry, the stencil can rest directly on the surface. If it is soft and/or moist, hold the stencil about an inch (2.5 cm) above the surface and proceed with instructions. When finished, remove the stencil or design pattern carefully, without disturbing the garnish.

Display Most of the garnishes in this book can be displayed up to four hours (see specific recipes for exceptions) if you are presenting them for a sit-down dinner party or buffet. However, they should be kept away from air and heat. Vegetables should be misted periodically with cold water to help keep them from drying out. If you are using them on hors d'oeuvres trays that are rotated regularly, lightly cover the garnishes with plastic wrap in between servings.

Blanching and Refreshing Fresh vegetables have brilliant color. The best way to maintain this color—and, in some cases, make it more vivid—is to blanch the vegetable. Some fruits can be blanched, but this is much less common. You blanch a vegetable by immersing it in boiling water for about a minute. Blanching is important because it makes the vegetable more pliable and easier to work with. Blanching also makes a vegetable more tender. Refresh the blanched vegetable immediately by draining it in a colander and then rinsing it under cold running water until it is cool. This technique halts the cooking process, so the vegetable does not become overcooked and the color is sealed in.

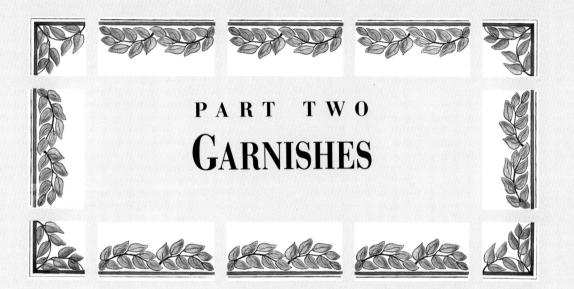

PART TWO
GARNISHES

CHAPTER THREE

THE VEGETABLE GARDEN

- SUN-DRIED TOMATO BRIDGE CUTS • POLENTA BASKET •

- ABSTRACT RED CABBAGE WISPS • CORN FLOWERS •

- MINIATURE TOMATOES • TEX-MEX TORTILLAS •

- SNOW PEA SEAGULLS • PINK POTATOES •

- ZUCCHINI AND YELLOW SUMMER SQUASH RIBBONS •

- AVOCADO BALLS • SQUASH AND ZUCCHINI ZIGZAG •

- LILLIPUTIAN CARROT BUNCHES • CUCUMBER CHAIN •

- RADISH MUSHROOMS • CORN-SILK NEST •

- DEEP-FRIED MATCHSTICK VEGETABLES •

- TRICOLOR BELL PEPPER FISH • PLAID PASTA •

SUN-DRIED TOMATO BRIDGE CUTS

*U*se this simple yet sophisticated garnish to decorate hors d'oeuvres or individual salads. It is also an excellent garnish for cheeses, such as a young, creamy, white goat cheese, and slices of fresh mozzarella. The small size of this garnish makes it perfect to float on top of a bowl of consommé, as the dark red of the tomato provides a stunning contrast to the clear, light-colored broth. Sun-Dried Tomato Bridge Cuts also work well as a delicate garnish for the top of tea sandwiches, which are especially nice to serve during a game of bridge.

You will need sun-dried tomatoes and aspic cutters. With small cutters, one sun-dried tomato will yield about 8 to 10 shapes.

▪ Cut open a whole, drained, sun-dried tomato packed in oil, and spread it out. Place the cut side down onto a cutting board. Disconnect the two halves, and use a paper towel to lightly blot the tomato to remove any excess oil. Leave a slight sheen to help prevent the garnish from drying out and to provide a lovely, glossy appearance.

▪ Remove and discard any seeds from the underside of the tomato halves. Using your fingers, press down the tomato halves and rub the surface to smooth them and make them as flat as possible.

▪ Use tiny aspic cutters with a playing-card theme to cut out pretty shapes from the tomato halves. Aspic cutters that are ½ inch (1 cm) long with about ½ inch diameter work well. Cut each shape closely to the last cut to use as much of the tomato as possible. If the cutters do not cut through completely, then use very small scissors with a fine tip or a very sharp knife with a fine blade to follow the design and finish cutting out the shape.

POLENTA BASKET

$\boldsymbol{P}$*olenta, a custardlike cornmeal preparation, is a specialty of Venice and northeastern Italy. Not only is polenta extremely tasty, but it is also a very versatile food. Polenta is adaptable to many forms of garnish and is a suitable embellishment for a variety of savory foods. It can be flavored according to the dish you have prepared by adding such seasonings as fresh herbs, crushed garlic, and freshly grated Parmesan or simply by using butter, salt, and pepper.*

It is great fun to make designs from shapes of polenta that match the theme of the food to be garnished. For instance, use polenta in the shape of a sailboat to garnish a seafood meal or shape it into a flower to garnish a garden salad. Polenta can also be served alone—for example, cut it into the shape of a house and serve it as an appetizer. For this project, I have chosen a basket shape because it is adaptable to many food themes. The size of the basket is only limited to the size cookie cutter you use.

You will need a 9-ounce (250-g) box of quick-cooking, instant polenta to make 2 baskets (using the dimensions given).

■ Lightly grease the sides and bottom of a shallow baking pan. A pan with the dimensions $13^{1}/_{4} \times 9^{1}/_{4} \times {}^{5}/_{8}$ inches (33 $\times$ 23 $\times$ 1.5 cm) works well.

■ Prepare the polenta according to the package directions. Flavor the polenta with desired seasonings, and working very quickly, spread the cornmeal mixture evenly into the prepared baking pan, smoothing the top with a spatula or knife. The mixture should be smooth, but if you

Cut out 7 diamonds and a basket handle (see page 125) from the polenta.

Cut each diamond in half to make 14 triangles of the same size.

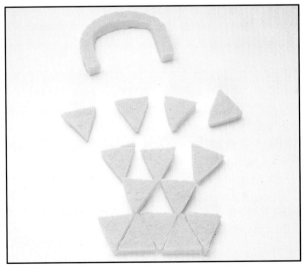

Arrange the polenta pieces in the shape of a basket (see page 125).

find any lumps, remove and discard them. Let the polenta stand at room temperature until firm enough to slice and cool enough to handle (about 30 minutes). Then tightly cover the pan of polenta with plastic wrap, and refrigerate until ready to serve.

■ Select a diamond-shaped cookie cutter in a size that you enjoy using. I prefer a cutter that creates 2 triangles (when the diamond is halved) that have ½-inch- (1-cm-) long sides. Using the cutter, cut out 7 diamond shapes from the polenta. Cut each shape very close by the last one to use as much of the polenta as possible. You should have polenta left over to make a handle later.

■ Using a knife, cut each diamond crosswise along the center to make 14 triangles of the same size. Dip the knife periodically in a bowl of hot water, so it will cut clean edges. Trim a slice of the polenta triangles along the bottom, to make all the triangles the same thickness, so that the basket will be of an even height.

■ The basket handle is made from a separate piece of polenta. Make a template from the pattern on page 125, and cut out a basket handle (see page 38 for directions on making a template). The basket container is made of 9 triangles; the basket base consists of 5 triangles. Arrange the polenta triangles according to the pattern on page 125. Make sure that the points of each triangle that form the basket container just touch, so that the negative (empty) spaces between the triangles also form triangles of equal size. The triangles that make up the base of the basket should be flush against each other, so that they appear to be one solid shape.

■ Attach the basket handle so that the ends of the handle begin at the inside corner of the outer left and outer right triangles of the top row.

■ This garnish is best when made just before serving. If made beforehand, wrap tightly with plastic wrap to prevent it from drying out and refrigerate it. Bring to room temperature before serving. The garnish can be decorated further with pieces of fresh herbs, such as chive blades, or other edible ornaments of your choice.

ABSTRACT RED CABBAGE WISPS

*T*he dappling of color and fabulous shapes of thinly shredded red cabbage create a natural garnish. Abstract Red Cabbage Wisps look marvelous sprinkled on top of salads or gracing a bowl of chilled soup, especially a light-colored soup such as vichyssoise (chilled cream of potato and leek soup). Though the flavor of cabbage can be strong when cooked, raw cabbage used in small quantities has a very delicate flavor.

**You will need a small head
of red cabbage.**

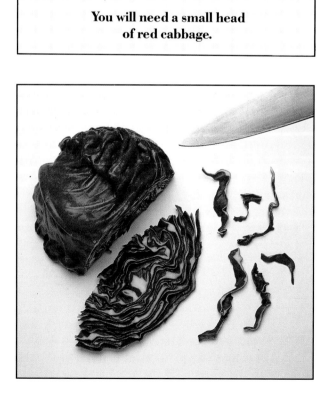

■ Remove and discard the tough outer leaves, and cut the cabbage in half. Then remove and discard the core.

■ Place a cabbage half, cut side down, on a cutting board and neatly cut into very thin slices, each about 1/16 inch (1 mm) thick, as uniform in thickness as possible. Using your fingers, separate the wavy pieces of cabbage from each slice. (Do not blanch this garnish, because the red cabbage loses its vivid color and the contrast between the white and red areas becomes less discernible.)

CORN FLOWERS

This versatile garnish can be used to decorate hot or cold dishes, such as soups, salads, and party dips.

> You will need an ear of corn and some cherry tomatoes. One cherry tomato will yield 2 corn flowers. One 8-inch (20-cm) corn cob will yield about 32 corn flowers.

■ Choose a fresh corn cob of any variety that has smooth, shiny, unblemished kernels. Remove the husks. Trim off the pointed tip of the ear of corn.

■ Transfer the ear of corn to a deep heatproof bowl, and pour boiling water over it to cover. Let stand for 1 minute, then drain the corn in a colander, and refresh under the cold running water until cool.

■ Hold the corn firmly with one hand (so that it doesn't slip while you are cutting) and, using a sturdy, very sharp knife with a thick blade, cut crosswise into the end opposite the stem to make slices about ¼ inch (6 mm) thick. If the corn is difficult to cut, try using a sturdy serrated knife.

■ Select a firm but ripe cherry tomato. Cut a ⅛-inch- (3-mm-) thick slice crosswise from the rounded end, opposite the stem end. Cut as neatly as possible, so that the cut has a clean edge.

■ Place each tomato slice, cut side down, in the center of a slice of corn. Sprinkle a pinch of minced fresh parsley in the center of each flower.

MINIATURE TOMATOES

*M*iniature Tomatoes can be used in clusters to garnish buffet platters of cold sliced meats. They are suitable for garnishing individual plates of food for any meal of the day and are particularly appealing with omelettes.

For each garnish, you will need
1 cherry tomato and 2 basil leaves.

■ It is important to use firm, but ripe, unblemished cherry tomatoes that are as round as possible. For each garnish, using a very sharp knife with a fine blade, cut about a third of the tomato crosswise, from the rounded end, opposite the stem end.

■ Choose 2 very small basil leaves from the interior group of leaves on the very tip of a sprig of fresh basil; 1 leaf should be slightly larger than the other.

■ Arrange the leaves next to each other on the surface to be garnished. Place the tomato, cut side down, on top of the leaves so that they radiate from underneath.

TEX-MEX TORTILLAS

*T*hese whimsical garnishes are a perfect match for any food that has a Southwestern or South-of-the-Border influence, such as chili con carne or fajitas. They are a good choice to adorn an appetizer that may need some additional color, such as seviche (a Spanish dish of raw fish or shellfish marinated in lime juice). Tex-Mex Tortillas can also be deep-fried, served in a basket, and used to dip into the ever-popular guacamole or salsa.

You will need fresh tortillas, either yellow or blue corn, depending on your preference. Each tortilla will yield 2 to 6 shapes, depending on the size of the cookie cutter.

■ Place a short stack of corn tortillas on a plate, cover them with lightly dampened paper towels, and then wrap the entire stack in plastic wrap to prevent it from drying out while you are working.

■ Remove a tortilla from the stack and place it on a cutting board. Use a cookie cutter (or make a template from the patterns on page 124; see also page 38 for how to make a template) to cut out the shapes. Cut each shape close by the last cut to use as much of the tortilla as possible. If the cutter does not cut through the tortilla completely, then use a very small pair of scissors with fine tips or very sharp knife with a fine blade to follow the design and finish cutting out the shape.

SNOW PEA SEAGULLS

*S*now pea pods offer a very versatile garnish, due to their subtle flavor, bright green color, and crisp texture. Snow Pea Seagulls are a perfect garnish for most Asian dishes or any hot or cold seafood or chicken preparations. Make a number of the Snow Pea Seagulls and use them along with other vegetable garnishes as crudités (raw food, especially vegetables, eaten before a meal to stimulate the appetite).

You will need large, long, firm snow peas. Each snow pea makes 1 seagull.

▪ Gently pull back the leaves of the stem, then cut off the stem, leaving as much of the point of the pod intact as possible.

▪ Transfer the pods to a heatproof bowl, and pour boiling water over them to cover. Let stand for 1 minute, then drain in a colander, and refresh under cold running water until the vegetables are cool.

▪ Using a very sharp knife with a fine blade, slit each snow pea lengthwise, starting at the stem end and cutting along the center of the pod seam. Be careful to keep the side of your knife blade horizontal and parallel to the work surface, so that the tip of the blade does not puncture the sides of the pod. Cut along the length of the pod, but leave ½ inch (1 cm) uncut before the tip. Remove and discard the seeds.

▪ Spread open the pod, cut side up, being careful not to rip open the uncut end. Gently fold the right side of the pod over the left side to form a loop. Then pull the right side through the loop, under the left side, carefully pulling the pod into a loose knot. Slowly and gently pull the knot tighter. The pod should knot easily. The closed pod end will rip open slightly as you knot it, but do not let it rip completely or the pod sides will separate and the knot will break.

▪ Flip the garnish over, so that the tips point upward, and then gently slide the knot until it is centered and the ends are of an even length.

PINK POTATOES

*F*or this garnish, beet juice does double duty: Not only does it color the skin of the potato, but it also infuses the potato with a hint of beet flavor, which is a fabulous complement to the taste of the vegetable.

This unusual garnish is an exciting change from the common halved or sliced potato—the constant companion to a sirloin steak. Pink Potatoes are stunning fanned and served hot or cold with chicken, fish, or vegetable dishes. Or simply slice them crosswise at even intervals and serve them in the shape of a whole potato, but with a slight space between each slice. This garnish also makes a spectacular addition to a composed salad, such as the classic salad niçoise. For your next party, try them sliced, in place of bread for canapés.

> You will need 1 medium-size beet and 2 medium-size boiling potatoes for each garnish.

- Place a halved beet and 2 peeled boiling potatoes in a 2-quart (2-l) saucepan with 3 cups (72 ml) cold water to cover. Set the saucepan over medium-high heat and bring to a boil. Reduce the heat to low, and simmer for 15 to 20 minutes, or until the potatoes are tender throughout when tested by inserting a knife with a fine blade through their thickest part.

- Let the potatoes and beet stand in the liquid until it has cooled to room temperature. Transfer the potatoes, beet, and liquid to a medium bowl, cover tightly, and refrigerate at least 12 hours—preferably 24 hours (for a brighter pink).

- Drain and discard the liquid and beet. Wrap the potatoes in plastic wrap and refrigerate until ready to use. The potatoes can be served cold, or they can be wrapped in foil and reheated in a preheated 300-degree F (148-degree C) oven until they are heated throughout—do not let them brown.

ZUCCHINI AND YELLOW SUMMER SQUASH RIBBONS

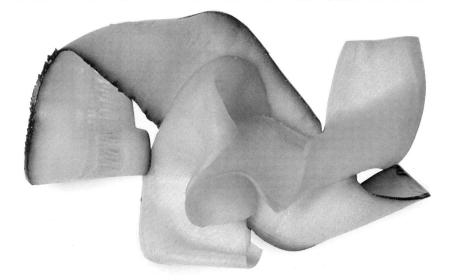

*M*ake a number of these vegetable ribbons, and use them as an accompaniment to other foods, such as roast beef or roasted chicken. They also look beautiful draped on food to lend it color and height. You might also use them as a zigzag border on large round or oval platters to frame the food being presented.

> You will need zucchini and yellow summer squash—judge the quantity based on how many garnishes you need and how large you wish each serving to be.

▪ Select a long, wide, unblemished zucchini and a yellow summer squash; each should have as uniform a thickness as possible. Trim the ends from the zucchini and squash. Cut off a thin slice of the zucchini along the bottom, so that it lies flat when inverted.

▪ Turn over the zucchini and, using a vegetable peeler, cut the vegetable lengthwise into long, thin strips from tip to tip. The strips should be as uniform in length and thickness as possible. Try to get a line of green (skin) on both sides of each strip. Repeat with the squash.

▪ Using a very sharp knife with a fine blade, trim the edges to straighten. Then trim the short ends of the strips to make them uniform in length.

▪ Transfer the ribbons to a heatproof bowl, and pour boiling water over them to cover. Let stand for 1 minute, then drain in a colander, and refresh under cold running water until the vegetables are cool. If serving as a side dish, cook and season as desired.

AVOCADO BALLS

*T*he skin from half an avocado makes a perfect container for this garnish. Avocado Balls have diverse uses: Set a container of them alongside a presentation of cold seafood or use them as an appetizer. Place a small cluster of the balls on food platters to add color or alongside a sandwich plate. Avocado flesh discolors rapidly, so this garnish is best made just before serving. A lemon bath will help slow down the discoloration process, but it will not prevent it.

For 2 filled containers, you'll need 2 ripe avocados, lemon juice, and lemon or lime zest or quartered citrus slices.

- Using a very sharp knife with a fine blade and starting at the pointed tip of a ripe avocado, cut lengthwise through the skin and flesh to the pit. Then run the knife all the way around the avocado. Holding the avocado in both hands, twist and separate the halves. Remove and discard the pit.

- Holding an avocado half firmly in one hand, use a melon-ball cutter to gently scoop a ball of flesh. (Rotating the scoop will help to make a "ball.") As you work, dunk each avocado ball in a bowl of undiluted fresh or bottled lemon juice to help prevent discoloration.

- When you have finished scooping balls from the avocado half, scrape out any remaining flesh. Then rinse and dry the cleaned-out avocado skin. Now you can fill the avocado "container" with the balls and top with lemon or lime zest or quartered citrus slices.

SQUASH AND ZUCCHINI ZIGZAG

*S*quash and Zucchini Zigzag is a geometric garnish meant to border a plateful of food. Accordingly, it works best on a round plate or platter. You can place the zigzag so that it forms a complete circle around the rim of the plate, or choose to create only a short zigzag pattern along the side. Squash and Zucchini Zigzag is a nice complement for meat or seafood.

> You'll need 1 zucchini and 1 yellow summer squash to garnish a small platter or a medium-size plate.

■ Use long, tender zucchini and squash. Only the skin of the vegetables is needed for this garnish, so choose vegetables with skins that are brightly colored and unblemished. Using a vegetable peeler, cut the skin of the vegetables lengthwise into fine strips that are as uniform in length and thickness as possible.

■ Transfer the strips to a heatproof bowl, and cover them with boiling water. Let stand for 1 minute, then drain in a colander, and refresh under cold running water until the vegetable skins are cool. Using a very sharp knife with a fine blade, trim the edges of the strips so that they are straight and further trim all the strips to uniform length and width. Two inches (5 cm) long by ½ inch (1 cm) wide are the best dimensions for most plates. But if a thinner or wider rim is to be garnished, change the dimensions of the strips accordingly.

■ Create a zigzag pattern, alternating between zucchini and squash. Continue this pattern, making sure the colors alternate, until the zigzag comes full circle.

LILLIPUTIAN CARROT BUNCHES

*T*hese small carrot bunches add vivid color to meat or vegetable dishes.

For each garnish, you will need 3 miniature carrots and 3 dill sprigs.

■ Select 3 miniature carrots, and trim the leaves but leave the green leafy base intact. Transfer to a heatproof bowl. Pour boiling water over them to cover. Let stand for 3 minutes. Drain in a colander, and refresh under cold running water just until the carrots are cool enough to handle.

■ While the carrots are still slightly warm, use a paper towel to rub the carrot surface vigorously to remove the thin layer of outer skin. If necessary, use a vegetable peeler, but do not cut into the surface of the carrot too deeply. Be careful not to break the carrot tip. Rinse under water, and blot dry with paper towel.

■ Choose 3 bushy branches of fresh dill sprigs with long stems. Using a very sharp knife with a fine blade, make a ¼-inch (6-mm) slit through the center of the top of each carrot.

■ Using your fingers or a toothpick, push the stem of each dill branch into the slit; to make it fit, you may have to bend or cut the stem. Rotate the carrots to hide the slits. Then gather the carrots into a loose "bunch," and arrange on the plate.

CUCUMBER CHAIN

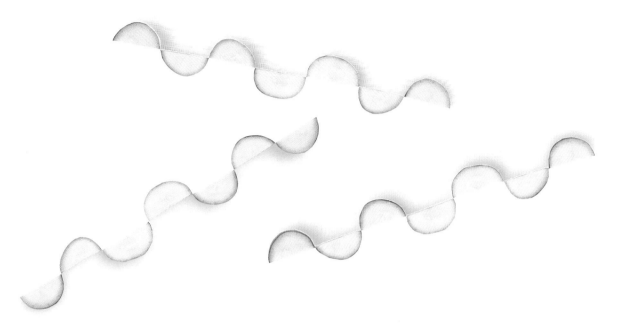

This lively garnish is a wonderful way to frame a food plate or platter. It works nicely for salad plates or arranged around a vegetable or seafood terrine. A tray of tea sandwiches or hors d'oeuvres would also be enhanced by a Cucumber Chain.

You will need a firm, unblemished cucumber with few seeds to garnish a small platter or a medium-size plate.

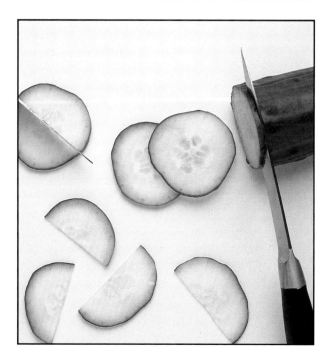

▪ Do not peel the cucumber. Slice the cucumber very thinly, then cut each cucumber slice in half crosswise.

▪ Choose cucumber halves that are as round and similar in size as possible. Lay a cucumber half onto the plate or platter to be garnished. This is the first "link" in the chain. Place a second half next to it, with the cut side facing the opposite direction. Continue this pattern until the chain is complete, making sure that each slice touches the end of the previous one, so that the green peel of the slices gives an appearance of a continuous wavy curve.

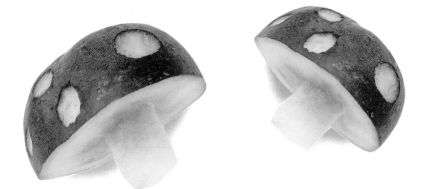

*R*adish Mushrooms add flair to pâtés, cold platters, and salads and are fun accompaniments for dips. I like to group them in a set of 2 to a plate, with 1 larger than the other; or in sets of 3 for a platter. Snip off the tips of a few fresh chive blades for "grass," and arrange them at the base of the "mush-rooms" for a finishing touch.

> **You will need large, unblemished red radishes. One radish will yield 1 radish mushroom.**

▪ A slightly oval-shaped radish is most effective for this garnish. Trim off the stems and roots, trying not to expose any of the white beneath the outer skin. Lay the radish on its side on your work surface, and holding it firmly, insert a corer

into the center of the stem end, two-thirds of the way up the length of the radish.

▪ Using a very sharp knife with a fine blade, slowly cut crosswise along the middle of the radish, just until the blade hits the corer. Do not cut right through the radish. If the blade does not hit the corer quickly, remove the knife and push the corer farther into the radish.

▪ With the knife held at this depth, rotate the radish 1 full turn, cutting along the middle of the radish. Remove the knife, and slide off the bottom half of the radish (the part surrounding the "mushroom" stem) and discard.

▪ Very slowly pull out the corer, while holding the radish firmly, being very careful not to break the "stem" of the "mushroom." Try pushing your finger through the base of the corer to separate the "stem" of the "mushroom" from the corer. Trim the red base of the "stem," so that the "mushroom" can stand up.

▪ Using a very sharp paring knife with a fine blade, slice an odd number of small circles, unevenly spaced, from the "mushroom cap" to expose the white underneath and simulate the spots on a mushroom. Cut the first circle where the roots were cut. Repeat the entire process with as many garnishes as you need.

CORN-SILK NEST

***N**estle a clutch of hard-boiled quail eggs, a peck of fresh-cooked miniature corn, or other appetizer or side-dish portion of food in this innovative garnish. The lustrous silk threads are a unique embellishment for cold buffet platters or an hors d'oeuvres tray.*

For each garnish, you will need 1 ear of corn.

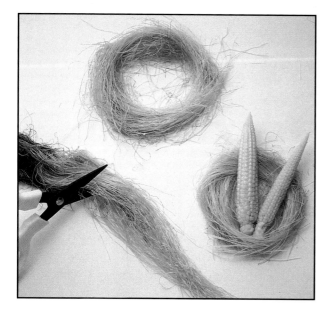

■ Carefully remove and discard the husks from an ear of corn of any variety. While holding the corn cob firmly at the stem end, gently remove the strands of silk attached to the cob by holding the clump of threads by the black ends and pulling toward you from the tip of the cob toward the stem end. Try not to tear or bunch the silk threads.

■ Gather the silk, keeping the threads parallel. Then separate into 2 equal bunches. Using a scissor, snip off the black ends.

■ Using both bunches end to end, form a loose loop about 3½ inches (9 cm) in diameter, resembling a nest. Snip off some of the longer, wild strands to shape the nest further, leaving some for a natural effect. Proceed to fill as desired. This garnish is best made the day you plan to serve it. To store, transfer an unfilled nest to a plate, cover lightly with a damp paper towel and then plastic-wrap and refrigerate.

DEEP-FRIED MATCHSTICK VEGETABLES

A loosely piled cluster of matchstick-size deep-fried beets, sweet potatoes, and potatoes is a scrumptious way to lend height to a plate of food.

> For garnish for 4 people,
> you will need 1 beet,
> 1 potato, and 1 sweet potato.

■ Peel a sweet potato and a potato, and reserve them in a bowl, covered with cold water, to prevent discoloration and to help remove excess starch. Then peel a beet and set it aside.

■ Using a mandoline, cut each vegetable into matchstick-size julienne, transferring the cut potato and sweet potato back to the bowl of water and reserving the beet matchsticks. If cutting by hand, make thin crosswise slices along the length of the potato, each about ⅛ inch (3 mm) thick. Stack 3 slices on top of each other and trim the

edges to straighten. Then cut lengthwise into fine, matchstick strips. Do the same with the remaining potato slices, transferring the matchsticks to the bowl of water while you are working. Repeat with the sweet potato and beet, transferring the sweet potato to the same bowl of water, and then reserving the beet matchsticks. Drain the vegetables in a colander, then roll them in paper towels to remove as much moisture as possible.

■ Meanwhile, heat 2 quarts (2 l) of vegetable oil in a 4- to 6-quart (4- to 6-l) pot over medium heat, until it reads 365 degrees F (185 degrees C) on a deep-fry thermometer. (Be careful to wear flameproof mitts to prevent fat burns!)

■ Toss the vegetables in 2 tablespoons (30 ml) of cornstarch to coat evenly, and then immediately deep-fry in batches for 30 seconds to 1 minute, or until crisp and golden brown. (It takes practice to judge desired doneness, and remember that the fries will continue to cook slightly even after they are removed.)

■ Remove with a slotted spoon or tongs to a paper-towel-lined cookie sheet to drain. Repeat with the remaining batches of vegetables. Lightly salt and serve hot. (Do not salt the vegetables before because the salt will break down the oil.) Keep warm (uncovered) in a low oven, or serve at room temperature.

TRICOLOR BELL PEPPER FISH

Use a school of these adorable bell pepper fish as a garnish to float on soup or alongside a seafood dish. They are especially appealing as a colorful accent for fried fish. The number of "fish" each pepper will yield will depend on the size of the cookie cutter or template you use.

You will need 3 different, brightly colored bell peppers, such as orange, yellow, and red. Each pepper will yield 6 to 10 shapes, depending on the size of the cookie cutter.

■ Remove the core from the top of each pepper by carefully cutting around the base of the stem as closely as possible. Twist and pull out the stem along with the core. Discard the stem and

core, but reserve about a teaspoon (5 ml) of seeds from one pepper to be used as eyes of the fish. Quarter the peppers lengthwise and rinse.

■ Lay the pepper quarters shiny side down on a work surface. Using a very sharp knife with a fine blade, run the blade away from you along the inside of each pepper to remove the white, spongy internal membrane and the excess pepper "flap" near the stem. Then run your knife flat along the underside of the peppers to remove about ¼ inch (6 mm) evenly across each. This contours the quarters, so that each lies flat and is of equal thickness. Try not to puncture the pepper through to the skin side.

■ Turn the pepper quarters over, so that the shiny side is up and the cut side is down. Press down on the pepper quarters with your palm to flatten them slightly.

■ Using a small fish-shaped cookie cutter or the pattern on page 125 as a guide to make a template, cut out fish shapes from the pepper. Cut out each shape as closely as possible to the last cut to use as much of the pepper as possible. If the pepper is difficult to cut, place a kitchen towel between the cutter and your hand, and shift your entire weight straight down onto the cutter. Dot each fish with a bell pepper seed for an eye.

PLAID PASTA

I have never met a person who does not adore pasta and is not familiar with at least twenty of the many pasta types. However, even the most knowledgeable of pasta aficionados will never have seen pasta like this! Enrobe fresh ravioli with this ultracolorful and flavorful pasta, or use it for lasagna noodles or tortellini wrappings. If you want to entertain imaginatively, plaid pasta is a must for your garnishing repertoire.

> **You will need egg, tomato, and spinach pasta dough; and some fine cornmeal.**

▪ Using a manual pasta machine, proceed with your favorite fresh egg pasta, tomato pasta, and spinach pasta dough recipes (kneading, resting, and so on) until they are ready to be rolled to the desired thickness for cutting. (In general, the wider the pasta shape, the thicker the pasta sheet should be; for example, fettuccine would be cut from a thicker sheet than linguine. However, some say the pasta should always be rolled as thin as possible, until it is translucent and you can see your hand through it, no matter what the shape will be. So, the thickness of the pasta is your choice.)

▪ Dust the egg pasta dough with fine cornmeal if it is too sticky to roll. Then, starting at the widest setting of a manual pasta machine, roll out a sheet of pasta. Continue to roll once through each setting down to a medium-thin thickness, 2 settings up from the thinnest. Cover the sheets with a layer of damp paper towel, roll up into a log and wrap in plastic wrap, and refrigerate until ready to use.

Roll out the egg pasta.

Place a few strands of spinach fettuccine onto the egg pasta sheet in straight, parallel rows.

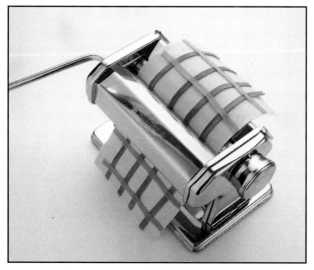
Lay a few tomato fettuccine strands crosswise in straight, parallel rows at the same intervals as the spinach.

■ Roll out the tomato pasta dough, and then spinach pasta dough once on each of the settings, from the widest setting to the thinnest setting, and then cut into fettuccine. Lay the fettuccine flat onto a cookie sheet, cover with a layer of damp paper towel, and then surround with plastic wrap. Refrigerate until ready to use.

■ Remove egg pasta from refrigerator. Working quickly, so the pasta does not dry out, start feeding the egg pasta sheet into the machine on 2 settings up from the thinnest setting, just to hold it in place. Remove spinach fettuccine from refrigerator and place a few strands lengthwise onto the egg pasta sheet in straight, parallel rows, at 1½- to 2-inch (3- to 5-cm) intervals, depending on how wide the sheet is and the look you want to achieve.

■ Slowly start to roll and feed in the sheet with the fettuccine. In between rolling, if the pasta gets too dry, sprinkle it very lightly with some water. If it is too sticky, dust with fine cornmeal. Keep the remaining pasta covered while you are working.

■ At the same setting, working quickly, start feeding in the sheet again, just to hold it in place. Lay a few tomato fettuccine strands crosswise in straight, parallel rows onto the sheet at the same intervals as the spinach.

■ Continue to roll the plaid pasta to the desired thickness. The more times you roll out the pasta, the wider the plaid stripes will be. Using a pastry wheel (for a zigzag edge) or a knife, trim the edges and cut the sheet as desired.

■ For variations you can cut the fettuccine so that it is wavy, or simply use pieces of other combinations of flavored (and colored) pasta, for the sheet and the pieces. Consult a pasta cookbook for pasta dough recipes. Some other pasta types that make interesting patterns include squid ink (black), beet (magenta), and carrot (orange).

CHAPTER FOUR

THE HERB AND SPICE RACK

HERB- AND SPICE-DUSTED PLATES

A simple and quick way to enliven a plate of food is to garnish the plate itself. You can decorate plates, platters, and bowls with seasonings that complement the food you are serving. Try minced fresh herbs, such as parsley for savory foods or mint for sweet foods. Breadcrumbs, freshly grated Parmesan cheese, or a mild paprika will also spice up a plate.

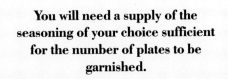

You will need a supply of the seasoning of your choice sufficient for the number of plates to be garnished.

■ Place the plate, bowl, or platter to be decorated on a sheet of waxed paper. Lightly coat the rim of the surface to be garnished with unsalted butter. Sprinkling or sifting the garnishing material, coat the prepared rim.

■ Using a dry paper towel, carefully wipe the interior and outer edges of the plate clean of any excess food, to give an even, finished appearance. Remove the waxed paper and brush off the bottom of the plate to avoid any tablecloth tracks.

Lemons

■ The same technique is applicable to lemon slices. Repeat the process above, dipping the prepared lemon slice or wedge into a saucer of the seasoning you have chosen. Red paprika is one example that makes an exciting contrast to the yellow lemon and is a superb garnish for seafood dishes, especially fried or en papillote (an individual serving wrapped in parchment paper).

CHIVE BRAIDS

*C*hive Braids are extremely versatile. You can scatter them in salads or use them to make a decorative border for plates. Try floating a few on top of soup just before serving it. They also add color and style to steak, baked potatoes, omelettes, and chicken dishes.

> **You will need 5 chive blades for each garnish.**

• Pick out 3 thick, long, fresh chive blades of similar size for the braid. Blades of about 8 inches (20 cm) or longer work well. Then select 2 more blades, slightly thinner and 5 to 6 inches (12 to 15 cm) long, for the ties. Trim off any excess shoots from the chives. Then trim the group of 3 to an equal length of about 7 inches (18 cm).

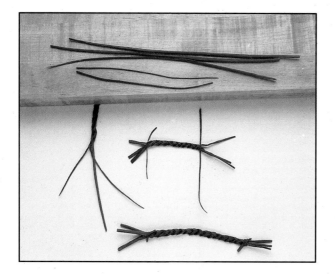

• Arrange the 3 chive blades parallel to each other on a work surface and 1 inch (2.5 cm) apart. Place a small, heavy bowl (for use as a weight as you braid the chives) as far up as possible on the root ends of the chives, to leave the chives exposed but firmly held down. Gently begin to braid a tight braid, being careful not to tear the chives. Continue braiding until there is an inch (2.5 cm) on each chive blade left unbraided.

• Slide 1 of the smaller, thinner chive blades under the bottom of the braid, and very slowly tie and gently pull it into a knot to close the braid.

• Using small scissors with fine points, snip the tie ends about ¼ inch (6 mm) from the knot. Remove the bowl and repeat the process with the other end of the braid and the remaining thin chive blades.

• Transfer the braid to a heatproof bowl, and pour boiling water over it to cover. Let stand for 1 minute, then drain in a colander, and refresh under cold running water until the braid is cool. Then trim the ends of the braid just to straighten them, leaving some length to resemble tassels.

HERB BASTING BRUSH

*E*veryone loves grilled food, and this garnish makes a perfect complement. If serving the food with a sauce, glaze, or additional marinade, you might wish to place the tip of the basting brush in a small pool of the sauce alongside the food, with the "handle" of the brush on the rim of the plate (so it does not get covered with sauce). The guests can then use the brush to "baste" the food with sauce as they eat. Make sure that you make a brush that is composed of herbs compatible with the sauce and the food to be garnished, because as the brush rests in the sauce it will slowly infuse the sauce with some flavor.

Use the freshest herbs possible, and choose at least one bushy herb. Fresh rosemary is pictured here, but other great herbs to use alone or in combination include the following: sprigs of fresh bay leaves, sage, thyme, dill, chives, and tarragon. (If using chives as a brush, use another herb, such as tarragon, to tie the brush.)

For each garnish, you will need about 7 small sprigs of bushy herbs, plus 1 chive blade.

■ Gather together a small group of fresh herb sprigs of your choice. Place a long, slender, fresh chive blade in a heatproof bowl. Pour boiling water over the chive, and let stand for 30 seconds. Then drain in a colander, and refresh under cold running water until the chive blade is cool.

■ Use the chive blade to "tie" a bunch of herbs, wrapping the blade 2 or 3 times around the bunch along where the stems begin. Gently knot the blade at the back of bunch. Trim the ends of the chive; take care not to trim too closely to the knot, or it might loosen. Place brush knot-side-down on the area to be garnished.

FLOWER AND MINT GARLAND

*R**emember making flower garlands as a child? This wreath is an edible spin-off of that favorite pastime. The Flower and Mint Garland is a bewitching and aromatic garnish that invites the onlooker to give a second, and then a third, look when it is displayed on top, alongside, or under a dessert. Use this garnish to embrace small portions of sorbet to refresh the palate between courses. Or exhibit it on an hors d'oeuvre, tea, or dessert tray.*

You will need a sprig of fresh mint and 3 to 5 flowers for each garnish.

■ In addition to mint, this garland can be made with any edible flowers (see page 121) or fresh herbs that you deem appropriate to the food to be garnished. For example, a garland made of a pineapple sage sprig and lemon-flavored marigolds would be an interesting and tasty match for a dish of pineapple sorbet.

■ Choose an unblemished, bright green, 7-inch (18-cm) sprig of fresh mint. (The longer the sprig, the larger the garland.) Place it on a work surface, and using a very sharp knife with a fine blade, make a slit about 1 inch (2.5 cm) from the root end of the sprig, taking care not to cut right through to either of the 2 ends of the mint sprig. Gently pull the other end (opposite the root end) through the hole of the slit to form a ring.

■ Push 2 or 3 short-stemmed flowers into the slit, so that the flowers are secure, visually balanced, and cover the hole. Gently push down the mint leaves in the arrangement desired. This garnish is best made the day you intend to serve it. To store, wrap in a damp paper towel, then loosely in plastic wrap. Seal tightly, and refrigerate until ready to serve.

HERBED CROUTON MONOGRAMS

Instead of a place card, use croutons to spell out a guest's name or initials. Be creative and cut out any design you want. Use these expressive morsels to decorate cheese trays or soups, to crown salads or hors d'oeuvres, or to accompany a dip. For a quick garlic bread, rub the cooked croutons with half a clove of garlic, then brush with melted herb butter just before serving.

> You will need 1 slice of white bread per letter, in addition to ¾ cup (20 ml) safflower oil, 4 tablespoons (60 ml) unsalted butter, and 1 tablespoon (15 ml) fresh thyme leaves or other herb per batch of 8 letters.

■ Use slices of very thick white bread with a tight crumb (the texture should be tight, with no large air holes). You will need about one slice per letter. Unless you are going to just cube the bread, I recommend using fresh bread, not day old, as letters and designs are slightly more intricate, and the bread needs to be cut easily. Pictured are croutons made from white bread, but you can use corn bread, rye bread, oat bread—you name it! Just make sure the choice of bread, herbs, and food to be garnished complements one another.

■ Remove all crusts from the bread. Using cookie cutters, cut out letters from the slices of bread.

■ Heat ¼ inch (6 mm) of oil in a large, heavy frying pan over medium heat until just bubbling. (Wear flameproof mitts to avoid fat burns.)

■ Meanwhile, in a small saucepan, combine some unsalted butter and fresh thyme leaves or other fresh herbs, and heat until the butter is melted. Any herbed butter you do not use can be refrigerated in an airtight container for up to 2 weeks.

■ Test how quickly the oil browns the bread by pan-frying a trimming from one of the slices. Add a batch of letters and pan-fry about 10 seconds per side, turning and stirring constantly, or until crisp and lightly golden brown. Remove with a slotted spoon or tongs, and transfer to a paper-towel-lined cookie sheet to drain. Remember: The croutons will still cook slightly after removal, so take that into account when judging the length of cooking time. Repeat with remaining batches.

■ Brush each of the letters with a touch of the hot, melted thyme butter just before serving.

HERB PUFF-PASTRY TWISTS

These fashionable herb-studded twists are a dependable garnish for a wide variety of savory foods, from soups to salads. This garnish can also be delightful for desserts, substituting cinnamon sugar for herbs. Frozen puff pastry is available in the freezer section of supermarkets. Just thaw according to package directions before using.

> **You will need a 17¼-ounce (483-g) package of puff pastry for 12-14 twists, and 4 tablespoons (60 ml) unsalted butter and 1 tablespoon (15 ml) fresh herb leaves per batch of 6 twists.**

■ Preheat the oven to 400 degrees F (200 degrees C). Roll the puff-pastry sheets on a lightly floured work surface to a ⅛-inch (3-mm) thickness. Cut into strips an inch (2.5 cm) wide and 12 inches (30 cm) long.

■ A strip at a time, press one of the ends to the edge of the long side of a lightly greased, shallow baking pan to secure. Holding that end firmly in place, start twisting the pastry strip by gently rotating it (in the pan) with your fingers away from you. Then press the other end to the opposite edge to secure. Repeat with the remaining strips, placing them 1 to 1½ inches (2.5-3.8 cm) apart. (Do not glaze the twists, or they will stick to themselves and will not keep their shape.) Bake in the preheated oven for 10 to 15 minutes, or until puffed and lightly golden brown.

■ Meanwhile, in a small saucepan, melt some unsalted butter and fresh herb leaves of your choice. Any remaining herbed butter may be stored in an airtight container in the refrigerator for up to 2 weeks.

■ Using a serrated knife, cut the twists from the pan, brush each with some of the melted butter and serve. This garnish is best made the day of serving. Store in an airtight container in a cool, dry place before basting with butter mixture. Do not refrigerate.

THE BOUQUET

FLOWER BLOSSOM BUTTER

*F*lower Blossom Butter can be used to adorn any food that would ordinarily be capped with butter. Vibrant swirls of flower petals and herbs are blended together to create a subtly flavored sweet creamery butter.

Whatever edible flowers and herbs you choose, aim for an aromatic and colorful combination that won't overpower the food it accompanies. Use a round patty of Flower Blossom Butter as a gorgeous garnish for such edibles as homemade muffins and breads. This garnish also makes a featherweight sauce—a glaze for steamed vegetables, fish fillets, or poached chicken breasts. For a surefire conversation piece at your next gala, pass a crystal plate of chopped ice holding disks of this exceptional butter.

For 1 log, you'll need 1 stick ($^{1}/_{2}$ cup, or 120 ml) unsalted butter, at room temperature; $^{1}/_{4}$ cup (60 ml) of assorted edible whole-flower petals (see page 121) and finely chopped fresh herbs.

Transfer the butter mixture to a rectangular sheet of waxed paper.

Push the pencil against the paper-covered butter cylinder.

Roll up the butter log and twist the ends closed.

■ In a small bowl beat the butter until soft. Gently fold in the whole petals and chopped herbs until well blended.

■ Transfer the butter mixture to a rectangular sheet of waxed paper. Form a cylindrical shape about 5 inches (12 cm) long and 4 inches (10 cm) from the sides. Fold the waxed paper just over the butter.

■ Place a long pencil against the paper-covered butter cylinder. Push the pencil against the butter, while holding the edges of the waxed paper in place. This movement helps form an even cylinder and removes air bubbles. Gently roll up the log of butter, and tightly twist the ends closed, being careful not to disturb the form. Wrap in two layers of aluminum foil and chill until firm enough to slice.

■ Unwrap and slice into ¼-inch (6-mm) thick rounds, slicing only what you need. Rewrap tightly and refrigerate again. Flower Blossom Butter can be refrigerated for up to 2 weeks or slipped into a freezer-proof plastic bag and frozen for 3 weeks.

TEATIME FLOWER SUGAR CUBES

This exquisite garnish was inspired by those dainty French sugar cubes that are decorated with finely piped frosting flowers. The main difference is this garnish uses the real thing. Teatime Flower Sugar Cubes make the perfect cup of tea even more perfect—not only are they picturesque on the saucer, but when dropped into the tea, they perfume the brew and then decorate it when the flowers float to the surface. You can also serve them with hot or iced tea or homemade lemonade.

You can use any type and shape of sugar cube you want, but white sugar cubes with a bridge-game theme work nicely; they are available in specialty food stores. Choose edible flowers that are an appropriate scale in relation to the sugar-cube size. Some flower blossoms contain miniature flowers—pull them apart and explore. If you want to use a larger bud with no stem, trim off some of the base to help the flower stand upright.

> You will need one egg white, 1 tablespoon (15 ml) superfine, or "bar," sugar; a selection of whole, small edible flowers (see page 121); whole, small, fresh mint leaves; plus the sugar cubes. (Each cube uses 1 flower and 1 or 2 mint leaves.)

- In a small mixing bowl, beat together the egg white and superfine sugar on high, or whisk for about a minute, or until it forms a small-bubbled, tight foam.

- Using your fingers or tweezers, dip the flowers and leaves 1 at a time into the egg mixture until evenly coated. Transfer to the surface of a sugar cube and arrange.

- Using a small, dry, clean pastry brush, brush off any excess foam, leaving only a sheen to adhere the flowers. Let the cubes stand at room temperature for 2 hours, or until the glaze is dry. This garnish is best made the day of serving. To store, place the cubes in an airtight container in a cool, dry place. They will last about 3 days. Do not refrigerate or stack the cubes, but keep them in a single flat layer.

SAVOY CABBAGE LEAVES

*S*avoy *cabbage works best for this garnish due to its wrinkled, ruffled appearance, but other types of cabbage can be used as well. For example, red cabbage will create a more unusual leaf effect. The natural curve, spring green color, and white-vein patterns of savoy cabbage make a very realistic leaf. A pair of slightly different-size leaves used along with some brightly colored edible flowers, such as nasturtiums, makes an alluring garnish for any savory dish or salad or can be arranged in clusters on a platter.*

> **For each garnish, you will need**
> **2 savoy leaves and**
> **1 or 2 edible flowers.**

■ Remove the tough outer leaves of a small head of savoy cabbage. Choose 2 unblemished, tender leaves that show a vivid contrast between the white veins and green background.

■ Place a leaf dull side (the exterior of the leaf) down. Using a very sharp knife with a fine blade, and starting at the base of the stem, cut the shape of a leaf freehand, making the stem the center and using the branching formation of the veins as a guide. Trim the base of the stem to straighten. Repeat with the remaining cabbage leaf, cutting it to a slightly smaller size.

■ Transfer the leaves to a heatproof bowl, and pour boiling water over them to cover. Let stand for 2 minutes. Then drain in a colander, and refresh under cold running water until the leaves are cool. Pat dry with a paper towel, transfer the leaves to the surface to be garnished, and center 1 or 2 edible flowers between the leaves (see page 121 for list of flowers).

SUGAR-DUSTED FLOWERS

This charming garnish enlivens a tea tray, a dish of homemade candies, or any other sweet ending to a meal. Consider using a large group of Sugar-Dusted Flowers for a centerpiece on a table or wedding cake. The same technique works well on fruits, such as fresh red currants. Just wash the fruit well and dry. (During the Christmas season, use this method to decorate freshly cut holly and berries for a gorgeous arrangement for the mantel or stairwell banister—but make sure everyone knows that holly and berries are not edible).

You will need 1 egg white, a tablespoon (15 ml) of superfine, or "bar," sugar; plus more to dust with; a selection of whole, small edible flowers (see page 121); and whole, small, fresh mint leaves.

- In a small mixing bowl, beat together the egg white and sugar on high for about a minute or until it forms a small-bubbled, tight foam.

- Using your fingers or tweezers, dip the flowers and leaves 1 at a time into the egg mixture until evenly coated. Transfer, stem side down, to a wire rack on a cookie sheet.

- Using a small, dry, clean pastry brush, brush off any excess foam, leaving only a sheen.

- Using a fine-mesh strainer, sift a light, even layer of superfine sugar onto the flowers and leaves. If any parts are not coated, paint on more egg mixture and sift with some more sugar. If you want the bottoms of the flowers and leaves coated, press the items in a bowl of superfine sugar before sifting the top surfaces with sugar. Let the flowers and leaves stand at room temperature for 2 hours, or until the glaze is dry. This garnish is best made the day of serving. To store, place in an airtight container in a cool, dry place. This garnish can be stored up to 3 days. Do not refrigerate or stack the flowers and leaves, but keep in a single flat layer.

EDIBLE-FLOWER ICE CUBES

Depending on the type of beverage to be garnished, ice cubes can be decorated with edible flowers, fresh herbs, fruit, a variety of liquids, and even vegetables. Use only the choicest of foods, because when the ice melts the guest will be eating the contents of the cube. Also, if you use more than one food, choose items whose color and flavor are appealing when combined.

> **You will need a supply of edible flowers, herbs, fruits, or vegetables.**

▪ Plain or delicately tinted (with food coloring) water works best. You can also make ice cubes out of liquids other than water, such as lemonade, ginger ale, coffee, or any kind of fruit juice. You will also need whole blossoms or petals of edible flowers (consult page 121 for a list). Any fresh herb leaves or sprigs will do; however, a less woody-stemmed herb is best, such as mint, tarragon, basil, parsley, or thyme. Avoid using rosemary or sage as they tend to be too overpowering for most beverages. Small slices of any fruit will do or zest from any citrus. As for vegetables, you must again be careful to match the beverage with the garnish: For example, an ice cube studded with half of a cherry tomato, sliced celery, and a sprig of thyme would make an ideal garnish for a Bloody Mary. Similarly, peach slices in peach juice would be perfect in a Fuzzy Navel.

▪ Fill an ice-cube tray about one-third full with water or other liquid. Freeze until ice crystals just begin to form (about 15 minutes). Add the garnish in the arrangement desired. Add more cold liquid to fill the cavities three-fourths full, and freeze until frozen solid.

SQUASH BLOSSOM TEMPURA

*S*quash Blossom Tempura can be made from pumpkin or zucchini blossoms. Closed, tight blossoms work best. It is a very festive garnish, because frying the closed blossoms causes them to burst open slightly to reveal the bright orange petals. Though tempura is traditionally served with a soy-based dipping sauce, this tempura does not need one. However, if you would like to serve it with a sauce, sprinkle it with a small amount of garlic butter just before serving, or have some on the side.

This is a garnish that must be made just before serving, so that the crispy coating does not become soggy. The tempura batter provides a very light coating, to best display the outlines of the stunning blossoms. Serve as an appetizer or as an accompaniment to any Asian or vegetable dishes.

For about 8 to 10 garnishes, you will need ⅓ cup (80 ml) all-purpose flour; 2 tablespoons (30 ml) cornstarch; ½ teaspoon (3 ml) baking powder; 1 egg yolk, lightly beaten; ⅓ cup (80 ml) ice water; 2 quarts (2 l) safflower oil; and about 8 to 10 squash blossoms.

■ In a medium bowl, combine the flour, cornstarch, and baking powder, and blend well. Stir in the egg yolk, and then add the water and mix until well blended. Place the bowl of batter in a larger bowl of ice water to keep it chilled while you are working.

Ingredients for Squash Blossom Tempura.

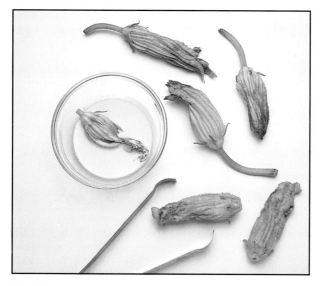

Dip the blossoms in the batter until they are well coated, and shake off excess.

■ Heat safflower oil in a 4- to 6-quart (4- to 6-l) pot over medium heat, until it reads 350 degrees F (185 degrees C) on a deep-fry thermometer. (Be careful—wear flameproof mitts to help prevent fat burns.) Meanwhile, remove the stems from the blossoms. Then rinse the squash blossoms and drain. Roll in paper towels to remove the maximum amount of moisture.

■ Dip the blossoms in the batter until they are well coated, and shake off excess. Deep-fry in batches of 3 or 4 at a time, so that the oil maintains the proper temperature. Fry, turning constantly, for about 1 minute per side, and no longer than 3 minutes total, until blossoms are puffed and crisp. The blossoms will continue to cook slightly after removing, so take that into account when judging doneness. They should be crispy with a light, airy coating, but not browned.

■ Remove with a slotted spoon or tongs, and place on a paper-towel-lined cookie sheet to drain. Repeat with remaining blossoms and batter. Serve at once, alone or with garlic butter.

Note: Skim the oil frequently to remove batter drippings, to keep the oil fresh, and to prevent it from darkening. Discard the oil when cool—once used for tempura, oil should not be reused.

PETAL PASTA

*T*his *breathtaking garnish looks complicated and time-consuming to make, but it is actually a cinch. Petal Pasta can be used to make many pasta shapes or the simplest of pasta cuts, such as fettuccine. Basically, this garnish lends itself to anything you would ordinarily use pasta for (even in place of wonton wrappers for soup), with the exception of baked dishes, because the flowers will turn too dark.*

> **You will need fresh egg pasta dough, some fine cornmeal, and a supply of edible flowers and fresh herbs.**

▪ Using a manual pasta machine, proceed with your favorite fresh egg pasta dough recipe (kneading, resting, and so on), until it is ready to be rolled to the desired thickness for cutting.

▪ Dust the egg pasta dough with fine cornmeal if it is too sticky to roll. Then, starting at the widest setting of a manual pasta machine, roll out 2 sheets of pasta. Continue to roll each sheet once through each setting, down to the thinnest setting. Cover the sheets with a layer of damp paper towel, roll up into a log and wrap in plastic wrap, and refrigerate until ready to use.

Scatter the flowers and herbs onto 1 sheet of the egg pasta.

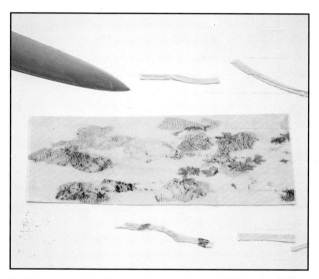

Roll the sandwiched pasta sheet to desired thickness, trim, and cut to desired dimensions.

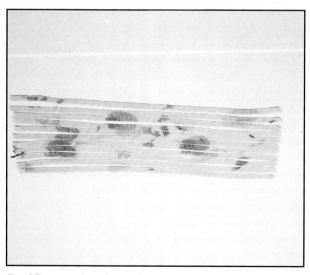

Petal Pasta cut into fettuccine.

- Select an assortment of edible flower petals, smaller whole blossoms, and fresh herb leaves. (See list on page 121 for edible-flower possibilities.)

- Scatter the flowers and herbs onto 1 of the sheets of pasta. Rub the edges of the sheet with some water, and place the second sheet on top. Press down gently on the pasta with your palms to seal in the flowers and herbs.

- Carefully transfer the sandwiched sheet to the pasta machine set at 1 below the thinnest setting. Working quickly, so the pasta does not dry out, carefully feed in the petal pasta, while rolling. If the pasta gets too dry in between rolling, lightly sprinkle it with some water. If it is too sticky, dust with fine cornmeal.

- Roll the pasta sheet again twice on the thinnest setting. Continue to roll the petal pasta to desired thickness (depending on how you will be using it). The more you roll out the pasta, the larger the shapes will be. Using a pastry wheel (for a zigzag edge) or a knife, trim the edges and cut the sheet to the size desired.

Creating Petal Purses

- A knockout presentation for Petal Pasta is to make little "beggar's purses." Cut out circles of petal pasta about 5 inches (12 cm) in diameter from a sheet of pasta, and then boil them until al dente (slightly firm to the bite).

- Place 2 tablespoons (30 ml) of a savory or sweet (such as fresh goat cheese) filling in the center of each circle, gather together the pasta at the top, and pinch together, wrapping the "purse" closed by gently knotting a blanched chive blade. Reheat in a covered dish in a warm oven, or serve at room temperature (depending on filling).

CHAPTER SIX

THE EXOTIC

- SAFFRON THREADS • CAVIAR GRAPES •

- CACTUS-PAD SERVING PLATE • SALMON ROSES •

- CHINESE NOODLE CAGES •

- GOLD AND SILVER PIXIE DUST •

- DOLLHOUSE MUSHROOM BASKET •

SAFFRON THREADS

affron is the word for the deep orange, pungent, dried stigmas of a particular blue- or purple-flowered crocus. In many cultures it has been used not only as a spice, but as a dye, a medicine, and an aphrodisiac.

> **You will need a pinch of saffron threads for each garnish.**

■ Sprinkle saffron threads on sauces or soups just before serving (so threads won't dissolve). The intensely colored, red-orange threads hold their shape and make a very delicate, lovely garnish. They are a marvelous addition to brightly colored foods, such as pumpkin soup, or to food that might need a color accent, such as clear broths and white cream sauces. As the threads dissolve, they add yellow color and pleasing flavor to foods.

CAVIAR GRAPES

Though salmon roe is not as prized as caviar (traditionally, the roe of a female sturgeon), it makes an enticing and exotic garnish. Always select eggs that have a fresh scent. The skin should glow and not look shriveled. Do not buy roe that has a milky or oily surface.

This lustrous garnish is well suited to grace hors d'oeuvres and pâtés, particularly those made of seafood. It is perfect for oysters on the half-shell. Note that heat will burst the eggs, so use this garnish for foods served cold or at room temperature only, and garnish just before serving.

For each garnish, you will need 5 or 7 salmon eggs of equal size, and 1 small piece of fresh dill.

■ Pick out 5 eggs for a smaller bunch, and 7 for a larger group of "grapes." Whatever the size of your bunch, always use an odd number of eggs. For a small bunch, place 4 eggs side by side in the shape of a square, and place the fifth below and between the bottom row of 2 eggs. For a larger bunch, arrange 6 of the eggs in a side-by-side rectangular formation, and place the last egg below and between the bottom row of 2 eggs.

■ Place a small sprig of fresh dill under the top row of eggs in the center. Arrange the grape clusters directly on the food or surface to be garnished to avoid moving the delicate roe unnecessarily.

CACTUS-PAD SERVING PLATE

*N*opales, or cactus pads, are parts of the Nopal cactus. They have a tender but crunchy texture, and their flavor is similar to that of string beans or asparagus, with an added tartness. Purchase cactus pads that are bright green and crisp. Larger pads will have fewer thorns and eyes, making them easier to work with. Once trimmed, they can be eaten raw or cooked—although for this garnish, they are not meant for this purpose. This garnish is a wonderful way to pass hors d'oeuvres for a party with a Mexican, Caribbean, or Hawaiian theme.

> **For each garnish, you will need 1 cactus pad and 2¼-inch- (6-mm-) thick slices of carambola (star fruit).**

▪ To prepare a pad for a serving plate, choose as large a pad as you can find, and with the tip of a knife remove the eyes and prickers from the area where you will place the food to be served. Try not to cut too deeply into the pad. Since this garnish is used only as a utensil and is not to be eaten, leave the prickers on the very outer edge of the pad. Trim the base of the pad for a neat edge.

▪ I like to garnish the narrow end (near the base of the pad) with a few thin crosswise slices from a long, narrow carambola. This fruit requires no preparation (other than washing) and has an exquisite flavor—a cross between plums and grapes. Arrange the food to be served directly on the pad.

SALMON ROSES

This dramatic version of a rose will bedazzle anyone and is a novel garnish to present with meat platters, seafood dishes, and salads or to highlight an hors d'oeuvres tray. The ornamental kale provides an elegant and edible backdrop for the pink salmon while adding an air of sophistication.

> **For each rose, you will need**
> **2 ornamental kale leaves**
> **and a ¹/₄-inch- (6-mm-) thick slice of**
> **smoked salmon about 8 inches**
> **(20 cm) long.**

■ Choose 2 unblemished ornamental kale leaves, 1 slightly smaller than the other, and trim the ends. The prettiest leaves tend to be located toward the center of the head. You can use either white kale with green edging or purple with green edging.

■ Slice a ¹/₄-inch- (6-mm-) thick slice of smoked salmon about 8 inches (20 cm) long (the longer the slice, the larger the rose). Then trim it to 1 inch (2.5 cm) wide. If it is not possible to slice 1 long piece, you can use 2 pieces joined together.

■ Starting with a short end, roll up the salmon in your fingers to form a cylinder to resemble the center of a rose. The salmon will adhere to itself so there is no need for toothpicks. Pinch the base of the cylinder lightly to help secure it. Continue to roll up the salmon (you are now adding more "petals"), by gathering and crimping the salmon and gently rolling back the edges to give a flowerlike appearance. Lightly squeeze the base of the rolled salmon rose to hold it together. Use the tip of a knife with a fine blade or a toothpick to help flare and distinguish the petals of the flower from one another.

■ Before serving, center the rose between the 2 pieces of kale. This garnish is best made the day you will be serving it. To store, wrap the individual roses loosely in plastic, seal tightly, and refrigerate.

CHINESE NOODLE CAGES

Chinese Noodle Cages add dramatic interest to any plate of food. The crunchy noodles encase the food in a dome shape, making a very becoming garnish for most savory foods, especially stir-fried dishes. I used uncooked fresh Chinese noodles, which are available at specialty food stores and Asian grocery stores. You can also substitute other uncooked fresh noodles. With the same basic method you can use more noodles to make a "nest" for presenting foods. Bird's-nest frying tools are available in several sizes, depending on your needs.

For 10 to 15 cages, you will need 1 pound (.5 kg) fresh Chinese noodles, 3 tablespoons (45 ml) cornstarch, and 2 quarts (2 l) safflower oil. (About 1 ounce (28 g) of fresh noodles will make 1 cage.)

▪ In a medium bowl, toss a pound (.5 kg) of fresh Chinese noodles with 3 tablespoons (45 ml) cornstarch (unless the noodles come already packaged and dusted with cornstarch). In the bottom half of a fryer basket, arrange the strands of noodles side by side, going in 1 direction. They should be arranged in a single layer, in evenly spaced 1-inch (2.5-cm) intervals.

In the bottom half of a basket, arrange the noodle strands.

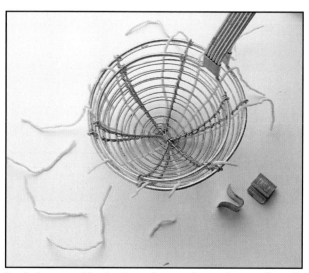
Lock the second basket into place, and trim the noodle ends.

Remove the top basket and, using a skewer, loosen the cage from the basket.

■ Meanwhile, heat 2 quarts (2 l) of safflower oil in a 4- to 6-quart (4- to 6-l) pot over medium heat, until it reads 365 degrees F (185 degrees C) on a deep-fry thermometer. (Be careful—wear flameproof mitts to prevent fat burns.)

■ Fit the second basket form over the noodles, pressing down firmly. Slide the lock into place over the 2 handles. Using scissors, trim the noodle ends to leave a 1-inch (2.5-cm) overhang. Turn the basket over, and trim any loose wisps hanging outside the basket mesh.

■ Place the basket upright into the oil until it is completely covered. Deep-fry for 1 to 2 minutes, or until noodles are crisp and lightly golden brown. The noodles will continue to cook slightly after removal, so take that into account when judging doneness. Transfer the basket to a paper-towel-lined cookie sheet to drain. Let stand for 1 minute for the cage to set.

■ Using scissors, trim the edges of the cage to the rim of the basket to align them, so that the cage can stand up. Unlock the handles and remove the top basket. Using a skewer, gently pry the cooked cage from the basket. Invert over decoratively arranged food on a plate. Repeat with remaining noodles.

Creating a Noodle Nest

■ Simply follow the directions above, but use more noodles and arrange them side by side with no spaces between them. To serve, lay the nest directly on a plate, and fill it with the food desired.

Note: Skim the oil frequently to remove any solid particles, to keep the oil fresh, and to prevent it from darkening.

GOLD AND SILVER PIXIE DUST

These glittering garnishes will add richness to any favorite sweet. Believe it or not, the gold and silver powder is edible!

You will need rolled sugar
cookie dough and edible
gold and silver dust.

■ On a lightly floured work surface, roll out dough to a $1/8$-inch (3-mm) thickness. Using crescent moon- and star-shaped cookie cutters, cut out cookie shapes.

■ Transfer the cookies to a cookie sheet, and bake according to directions. Let the cookies stand until cool, and then brush with a thin coat of gold and silver dust.

DOLLHOUSE MUSHROOM BASKET

*G*uests *will marvel at this amusing garnish, and mushroom lovers will especially adore it. A Dollhouse Mushroom Basket is literally and figuratively a mushroom basket, being made entirely of mushrooms. Make several baskets for picture-perfect garnishes for any beef or vegetable dishes.*

> **For each garnish, you will need
> 2 American short-stemmed
> mushrooms and 8 to 10 enoki
> mushrooms, 1 tablespoon (15 ml)
> lemon juice, and 1 blanched
> fresh chive blade.**

▪ For each garnish, choose 2 unblemished American short-stemmed mushrooms, as similar in size as possible. Twist off the stems and discard. You should now have 2 mushroom caps.

▪ Slice a ¼-inch- (6-mm-) thick piece crosswise from the center of the first mushroom cap, reserving the rest of the cap for another use. Using a very sharp knife with a fine blade, trim the glands (the dark, fanlike part) and discard. Then trim the ends of the slice evenly so it can stand up. This is the handle of the basket. Brush lightly with fresh or bottled lemon juice to help prevent discoloration and reserve.

▪ With a small spoon, scoop out some of the center of the second mushroom cap, being careful not to go through the bottom. The cap should be just slightly hollowed, so there is room for the enoki mushrooms to stand up. This is the basket. Brush it with fresh or bottled lemon juice to help prevent discoloration.

▪ Dip a group of about 8 to 10 enoki mushrooms in lemon juice, and blot dry with paper towel. Slice the stems from the cluster of enoki mushrooms, so the mushrooms are about ¼ to ⅓ inch (6 mm to 8 mm) tall. Select a variety of sizes, some with larger caps than others, for a more realistic-looking group. Using tweezers or your fingers, fill the mushroom basket base with the enoki until full. Place the handle on the edge of the basket across the center. (It should balance and stay in place of its own accord. If it doesn't, trim the edges again to even them.)

▪ Using a small pastry brush, gently dab the basket with more lemon juice, being careful not to disturb the enoki mushrooms, and serve at once. The baskets can be served with or without a handle. If desired, tie a blanched fresh chive blade around the handle to form a bow. Allow the ends of the bow to drape down; trim the ends of the chive just to even.

CHAPTER SEVEN

THE SWEET SHOP

- KUMQUAT POSIES • PINEAPPLE SHOOTING STARS •

• FAIRY TALE CANDY • SUGAR COOKIE GIFTS •

• MINIATURE WATERMELON SLICES • BANANA ARCHES •

• SWEET LACE • MARBLED SCROLLS • CHOCOLATE PAINT •

• DARK CHOCOLATE AND WHITE CHOCOLATE PLASTIC •

• CHOCOLATE PRETZELS • MARZIPAN CONFECTIONS •

• STRAWBERRY RUFFLES • EGG YOLK PAINT •

• PIECRUST STYLES • STAINED-GLASS COOKIES •

• GRILLED FRUIT KEBABS • CANDY SUSHI •

• WHOLE ALMOND BARK •

KUMQUAT POSIES

*K*umquats are entirely edible. The brilliant orange skin is tender and sweet, and the pulp is wonderfully tart, with an orangelike flavor. Kumquat Posies make an upbeat garnish for poultry, stuffings, salads, muffins, and desserts. Their visual appeal and flavor work especially well with duck and are a terrific accompaniment to pork.

For each garnish, you will need 1 kumquat with leaves.

• Choose a firm, plump, unblemished fruit with leaves, if possible. If you cannot find fruit with leaves, substitute fresh bay leaves and use as a dessert garnish. Cut a fruit in half lengthwise, through the center and down the sides, but not through the bottom layer of skin. Then cut it in half crosswise, through the middle of the kumquat across the first cut, but again not through the bottom layer of skin.

• Gently push down the "petals" of the kumquat so that they flare open. You might need to cut slightly further along each cut to help the petals separate, but do not break the skin at the center of the base that holds the fruit together.

• Turn the fruit over, and gently press down on the center of each petal to flatten it slightly (they should remain rounded over the fruit underneath). Though it is not absolutely necessary, you can remove any seeds from the fruit with the tip of a knife before serving.

• Arrange 2 leaves underneath the posy, and use the posy alone or along with several posies of varying sizes in a cluster.

PINEAPPLE SHOOTING STARS

Pineapple Shooting Stars bring a color boost to any dish. Use these appealing garnishes to enliven salads, fried foods, food platters, desserts, or Asian dishes. Alternatively, echo a platter border with a string of shooting stars for a breathtaking presentation.

For 10 to 15 garnishes, you will need a ripe, fresh pineapple with its leaves.

- Using scissors, cut a long, unblemished, green frond from a pineapple. Trim the end opposite the point at an angle.

- Peel and core the pineapple. Cut a ³/₄-inch- (2-cm-) thick slice lengthwise from the most yellow flesh of the pineapple. Trim along the bottom of the slice so that it lies flat. Using a star-shaped cookie cutter with about a 1¹/₂-inch (3-cm) diameter, cut out a star from the pineapple. Place the frond point underneath one of the star tips for the light streak. Repeat with the remaining pineapple; cut each star closely to the last cut to use as much of the pineapple as possible.

FAIRY TALE CANDY

*R*emember the tale of Hansel and Gretel? The Wicked Witch lived in a sugar-coated gingerbread cottage bedecked with glittering candy from every child's dreams. Just as those goodies lured Hansel and Gretel, you can use colorful and ornamental candies for garnishes that will appeal to even the most particular of sweet lovers.

> **You will need enough colorful and ornamental candies to accent your dessert.**

■ Two of my favorite candy garnishes are French candy seashells and ribbon candy (see source list, page 122). The ribbon candy can be used whole, under, on top, or alongside a dessert. It works especially well placed under a rectangularly shaped, ethereal puff-pastry dessert, such as a napoleon. Or use pieces or loops of ribbon candy or whole French candy seashells on ice cream or cake. Some other fun (and addictive) candies are chocolate-covered espresso beans and multicolored licorice strings.

SUGAR COOKIE GIFTS

***N**ot only are Sugar Cookie Gifts suitable for any dessert tray or at teatime, but children love these spirited garnishes. For a holiday theme, use red and green decorating gels or frosting.*

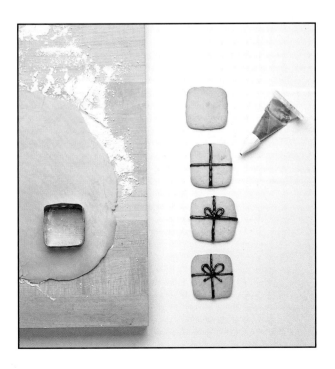

You will need the ingredients for your favorite rolled sugar cookie recipe, plus gel or frosting in appealing colors.

■ Follow the directions for the sugar cookies. Roll out the dough to a ¼-inch (6-mm) thickness, and cut out square and rectangular shapes. Bake according to the recipe. The cookies often have a puffy look, with slightly rounded sides. If you desire straight sides, just trim the edges of the baked cookie with a knife.

■ When the cookies are cool, decorate with colored gel (available in tubes fitted with a writing tip) or frosting in a pastry bag fitted with a writing tip. Pipe a straight, vertical line down the length of the cookie, through the center. Then pipe a straight, horizontal line across the cookie, through the center, and over the first line so that the lines (ribbons) intersect at the center of the cookie. Then pipe a "bow" design on the center of the cookie; the knot of the bow should be the point where the 2 ribbons intersect.

Miniature Watermelon Slices

*W*atermelon evokes images of summer picnics and childhood games on grassy pastures. Those pictures inspired this sprightly garnish. Miniature Watermelon Slices are very refreshing to eat and have a lot of visual appeal due to their compact size and the startling contrast of the ink-colored seeds with the lush, juicy, pink-red flesh. Arrange a few slices on a platter of fried chicken or other picnic fare. Add them as a finishing touch to an individual fruit plate, a complement to brunch foods, or a surprising addition to a cheese board.

You will need a ½-inch (1.25-cm) thick section of ripe watermelon for 10 to 20 garnishes.

■ Cut a ½-inch- (2-cm-) thick slice of watermelon. Place the slice flat on a work surface, and using a semicircular-shaped cookie cutter or a knife freehand, cut out a semicircular piece of watermelon from an area with a lot of seeds. Continue, cutting each shape closely to the last cut to use as much of the watermelon as possible. If you want more seeds in your garnish for sake of appearance, just remove a few seeds from another slice and push them gently into the surface of the garnish.

BANANA ARCHES

*U*se this garnish on a plate alongside a dessert or portion of salad, to partially surround the food. Alternatively, enclose the food entirely: Position two Banana Arches, so that the ends touch each other and the uncut sides face toward the center of the plate to form a circle. Place the food in the center of the circle. This garnish is an eloquent way to augment the beginning or finale of a meal.

For 4 garnishes, you will need 1 ripe banana.

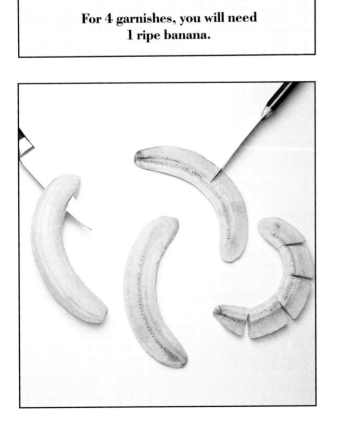

. Select a banana that is as curved as possible. It should be ripe, but not so ripe that it has many brown spots on its skin. Gently peel the banana, and trim the end opposite the stem. Slice the banana in quarters lengthwise, following its shape. Brush each slice with fresh or bottled lemon juice to help prevent discoloration.

. Then cut one of the banana slices in diagonal cuts widthwise in even increments, about 1½ inches (4 cm) apart. Work from the outside toward the inside curve. Take care not to cut all the way through to the inside curve; stop cutting at about ¼ inch (6 mm) from the edge of the inside curve. Very gently open up the slices to help them fan out and form an arch, but be careful not to tear apart the sliced banana—it will be very fragile. Repeat with the remaining banana slices.

SWEET LACE

*D*oilies are an instant stencil to create a delicate, lacy pattern on any flat surface. You can use any delectable sweet food that can be sifted or sprinkled to form the pattern. An entire doily can be used to transfer a pattern to the top of a cake to substitute for or augment a frosting. Or place a doily on a pan of brownies or other dessert that will be cut later.

You can also cut smaller sections of the doily—such as strips, triangles, minicircles, or diamonds—and sift a pattern onto an individual dessert portion. Quite often, I use this ready-made stencil to create a design directly on a plate, and then place a dessert treat on top of that.

You will need a doily and something sweet for sprinkling. Some heavenly foods to use for sifting include cocoa powder, confectioners' sugar, and a mixture of cinnamon and superfine sugar in a 1:2 ratio.

Using a Full Doily Pattern

▪ Lay a doily flush against the surface to be garnished. Sift the food onto the doily, until the entire doily is covered with an even layer. Then gently remove the doily, lifting it straight up, so as not to disturb the very fragile pattern. (If garnishing a plate, with the doily in place, use a dry pastry brush to brush away the excess food surrounding the doily; the surface should have a clean, finished appearance.)

Using a Section Doily Pattern

▪ Follow the directions above, but sift the garnishing material over the entire surface of the food to be garnished (both on top of and around the piece of doily). Then lift off the doily piece.

For an even more graphic, two-tone presentation, place pieces of waxed paper on top of select sections of the doily, and sift confectioners' sugar on the exposed, doily-covered areas. Then carefully lift off the paper, place it over the section just garnished, and sift cocoa powder on the remaining doily-covered areas.

MARBLED SCROLLS

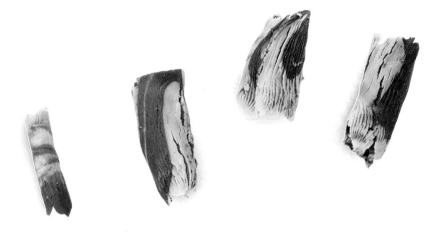

This is one of the many magnificent garnishes to make from chocolate and can be used to crown any dessert. The trick is to have both white and dark chocolate melted at the same time and to practice forming the scrolls. It is a difficult movement, and practice does make perfect.

You'll need white and semisweet chocolate, about 2 ounces (56 g) of each, coarsely chopped, to make 15 to 25 scrolls.

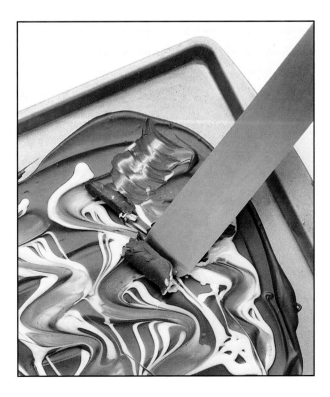

■ In the top of 2 separate double boilers, set over hot water just under a simmer, melt the white chocolate and the semisweet chocolate. The chocolates should melt very gently—if they are too hot, they will be flecked with light spots. Do not allow *any* water to drop into the chocolates. If it does, it is better to start over. Stir the chocolates frequently until they are just melted.

■ Remove the top of the pan from the heat, and immediately pour the white and dark chocolates onto a cool, smooth surface—marble or Formica works best. You can also substitute a shallow baking pan. Working quickly, spread them both at once, not blending them, but just lightly "marbling" them as you spread. Spread a very thin layer of chocolate, about ⅛ inch (3 mm) thick.

■ Let cool just until set. Do not let the chocolate harden completely—it should still be somewhat pliable. With a spatula or pastry scraper held at a 45-degree angle, press against the chocolate sheet, pushing away from you to form scrolls. The higher the angle and the thinner the chocolate, the tighter the curl. Serve at once, as marbled scrolls are very fragile and perishable.

CHOCOLATE PAINT

*Y*ou can draw anything with chocolate: fanciful shapes, flowers, animals, letters, numbers…the list goes on. Just melt some semisweet or white chocolate as per the directions on page 103. You can also make cups of chocolate to be filled with mousse or berries. For a truly elegant garnish, paint your favorite fruit!

You will need white or semisweet chocolate and a pastry bag.

Painting With Chocolate

▪ Fill a pastry bag half-full with melted chocolate. It is best to use a pastry bag with a plastic tip, not a metal tip, as the metal tip will cause the chocolate to harden. You can make a paper pastry bag by cutting a triangle of waxed paper with 1 longer side (to form an isosceles triangle). Holding 1 corner in your right hand, roll over to form a sharp point in the longer side of the triangle. Wrap the paper around to form a cone-shaped bag and tuck in the corner to secure. Fill the bag halfway, and snip the size of point desired. Alternatively, use a sturdy plastic bag as a pastry bag, and snip off a piece from a bottom corner for a hole.

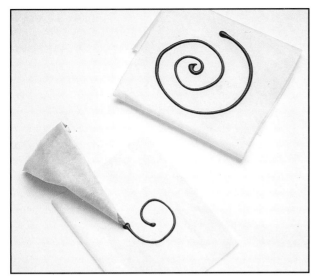

Pipe chocolate designs onto parchment paper.

Paint melted chocolate on the interior of foil baking cups.

Dip fresh fruits into melted chocolate and let harden.

■ Pipe chocolate designs directly onto cakes or other surfaces, or onto parchment-paper-lined cookie sheets, and refrigerate until hardened (about 3 minutes). Peel away the parchment paper, gently transfer the designs to the surface to be garnished, and serve at once.

Making Chocolate Cups

■ Use a small pastry brush to paint a smooth coat of melted chocolate on the inside of foil baking cups of any size (from candy to cupcake). Take care to get chocolate in between the pleated sides, but maintain the shape of the cup. Paint a little more on the inside rim to support the edge of the cup.

■ Transfer to a cookie sheet in its original shape and refrigerate until hard (about 3 minutes).

■ Apply a second coat of chocolate, and return to the refrigerator until it hardens. Use a skewer to pull back the paper from the edge, then peel. Fill around the cup, not from top to bottom, with dessert of your choice, and serve at once.

Painting Fruit With Chocolate

■ Just wash the fruit (fresh strawberries and cherries are delicious); dry well; dip in melted chocolate; transfer to a parchment-paper-lined cookie sheet and let harden for about 3 minutes in the refrigerator. Serve at once.

DARK CHOCOLATE AND WHITE CHOCOLATE PLASTIC

Chocolate plastic, or plastique, is a pliable, edible, chocolate mixture that is very versatile. It can be rolled, pinched, molded, cut into shapes, and made into almost anything. After trying this design, you may be inspired to create your own.

With this project, the chocolate is made into 2 beautiful and elaborate containers that can be filled or used to wrap around a dessert. Pipe mousse into a chocolate plastic container or use it to hold chocolate truffles. You can make the containers any size you want, but remember that although it is delicious, a little goes a long way—it is rich!

This recipe makes 2 garnishes. For white chocolate plastic, you'll need 4 ounces (112 g) of white chocolate, coarsely chopped, and 2 tablespoons (30 ml) of light corn syrup. For dark chocolate plastic, you'll need 4 ounces (112 g) of dark semisweet chocolate, coarsely chopped, and ¹/₄ cup (60 ml) of light corn syrup. You'll also need confectioners' sugar to dust your rolling pin.

For each chocolate:

• In the top of a double boiler, set over hot water just below simmering, melt the chocolate. The chocolate should melt very gently—remember, if it is too hot it will be flecked with light spots. Do not allow *any* water to drop into the chocolate. If it does, it is better to start over. Stir the chocolate frequently just until smooth—about 2 minutes.

• Remove the top pan from the heat, and immediately transfer the chocolate to a mixing bowl; let stand about 5 to 10 minutes, or until the chocolate is at room temperature, but not set. Beat in the corn syrup at low speed for 5 to 10 seconds, or until the mixture thickens and begins to lose its shine.

• Roll the mixture into a log shape, and wrap tightly in 2 layers of plastic wrap. Let set overnight at room temperature.

• The next day, unwrap the chocolate, and place it on a work surface that has been lightly dusted with confectioners' sugar. Knead until soft and smooth. If it is humid, the plastic will be sticky—knead in a little sifted confectioners' sugar.

• Break off 2 walnut-size pieces of dark chocolate plastic, and roll each into a 12-inch- (30-cm-) long rope, shaping them as evenly as possible.

• Break off a walnut-size piece of white chocolate, and roll it into a 12-inch- (30-cm-) long rope, shaping it as evenly as possible.

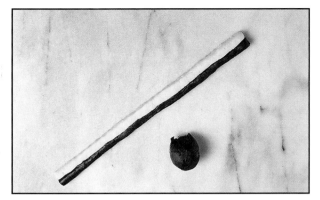

Lay the dark chocolate ropes on either side of the white chocolate rope.

Roll the chocolate plastic strip from left to right.

Gradually roll up the chocolate plastic to form a container.

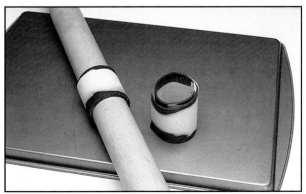

Trim the edges of the container so that it can stand up.

For the garnish:

▪ Lay the dark chocolate ropes lengthwise on either side of the white chocolate rope. They should be flush against one another, and as straight as possible. Press down on the ropes with your palm to flatten slightly. You should have enough plastic to repeat the process to make a second container. (To store any unused chocolate plastic, roll into a ball, wrap tightly with 2 layers of plastic wrap, and store in an airtight container at room temperature for up to 2 weeks.)

▪ Lightly dust a rolling pin with confectioners' sugar. Roll the chocolate plastic strip from left to right, to a $1/16$-inch (2-mm) thickness. Using a very sharp knife with a fine blade, trim the strip to a 10-× 2-inch (25-×5-cm) rectangle.

▪ Using a wide spatula and your fingers, carefully transfer to the back of a flipped-over shallow baking pan. Using a slightly damp paper towel, very gently wipe the surface of the chocolate plastic to remove any remaining confectioners' sugar. Place a sheet of plastic wrap directly on the chocolate plastic, and seal so it is airtight. Let stand at room temperature for 30 minutes.

▪ Unwrap the chocolate plastic, flip the plastic strip over (clean side down), and place the center of a rolling pin onto the plastic's short end and gradually roll it up to form a container. (The diameter size of the chocolate container depends on the diameter of the rolling pin itself. If you prefer a smaller or larger diameter, use your hands and roll freehand.)

▪ Slide the container off the rolling pin and, using scissors with fine points, trim the edges of the container to give a finished appearance and to ensure that the container can stand up. Choose which side you want to face the guest, because none of the sides will match exactly. If you are not using the container right away, wrap it in plastic wrap and store at room temperature. Place on a plate and fill just before serving.

CHOCOLATE PRETZELS

The ever-popular pretzel is back—but now there is a sweet version, with coarse sugar crystals replacing the salt! This is a striking garnish that can be used with any dessert with spectacular results. The pretzels do not have to be made from chocolate cookie dough—instead, try rolled sugar cookie dough. Or use both, twisting a rope of each ingredient together into a single rope, and then shaping the two-color rope into a pretzel, for a two-tone effect.

For each garnish, you'll need 2 tablespoons (30 ml) rolled chocolate cookie dough, a lightly beaten egg white, and coarse sugar crystals.

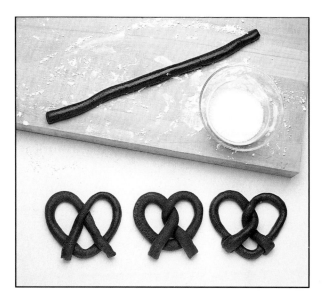

▪ On a lightly floured work surface (or one dusted with confectioners' sugar), roll the cookie dough into a 14-inch (35-cm) rope, as even in thickness as possible. (If you want a smaller pretzel, make a smaller rope.)

▪ Form the dough into a heart shape by bringing both ends of the rope upward, then curving the ropes in, so that the ends point downward. Then, place the right end of the rope over the left, twisting it around the other end once. Fasten the ends to the base of the "pretzel" by tucking them under the base and cutting off the excess. Repeat with the remaining dough.

▪ Carefully transfer the pretzels to an ungreased cookie sheet, placing them about 1 inch (2.5 cm) apart. Brush with egg white and sprinkle with the sugar crystals. Follow the baking directions for your rolled cookie recipe. Serve hot or at room temperature.

*M*arzipan is an edible paste made of ground almonds, sugar, and egg white. The tradition of shaping marzipan into animals, various foods, and other fanciful objects dates at least to the Middle Ages. Once colored with vegetable dyes, this paste can be used to represent almost any item you can imagine. I once attended a dinner party at which a very artistic hostess created marzipan portraits of each of her guests, and used them as place cards.

You can buy pre-made marzipan at specialty baking shops or supermarkets. Use marzipan confections to garnish desserts and dessert trays or as a centerpiece, such as a basket of marzipan strawberries or a cornucopia. Try making shapes—both serious and whimsical—other than the ones listed here.

> For each garnish, you will need 1½ tablespoons (22 ml) marzipan and food coloring in colors of your choice.

Making Marzipan Lemons

▪ Place a walnut-size piece of marzipan in a small bowl, and add a drop of yellow food paste with a toothpick. Stir until well blended, adding more color if needed.

▪ Roll the marzipan into an oval shape. Roll the marzipan oval along the raised, dimpled side of a grater, or make markings similar to lemon skin with a round wooden toothpick. Pinch each end lightly to make it resemble a lemon.

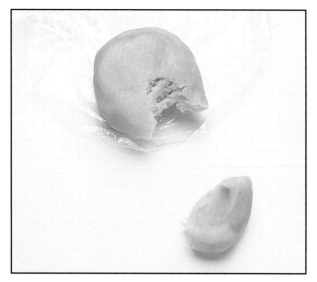

Break off a walnut-sized piece of marzipan.

Add a drop of colored food paste to the marzipan and blend.

Use toothpicks to make peel markings.

Making Marzipan Oranges

▪ Follow the directions for the lemon, but use orange food paste and form the marzipan into a ball. After making markings to resemble the peel, stick a whole clove in the center of the top of the orange.

Making Pea Pods

▪ Place a walnut-size piece of marzipan in a small bowl and add a drop of green food paste with a toothpick. Stir until well blended, adding more color if needed. Set aside one-sixth of the mixture.

▪ Shape the larger piece of marzipan into an elongated oval with dull pointed ends. Using a toothpick, score a smaller pod shape in the center of the marzipan, and scoop or hollow out the center.

▪ Use the remaining marzipan to make 4 small balls resembling peas. Arrange the "peas" in the center of the pod, and gently press down on the sides to secure.

Note: Although the vegetable dyes that you can buy in a supermarket work well, professional bakers' food pastes will give a more saturated, thorough color to marzipan and other foods. Always dye food with a minuscule amount, just a drop, then stir it in until it is well blended, adding more if needed. This way you will build up layers of color. Do not add too much in the beginning or you will overcolor the food, and it will look unnatural.

STRAWBERRY RUFFLES

Strawberry Ruffles make a pretty decoration for desserts, especially cakes and cupcakes. These garnishes can also enliven savory entrees, appetizers, and salads.

**For each garnish, you'll need
1 strawberry and 1 fresh mint sprig.**

▪ Select firm, ripe, bright red strawberries. For each garnish, cut an extremely thin slice from the very top of the strawberry, where the hull is located.

▪ Place the strawberry hull side down on a work surface. Make 4 lengthwise cuts along the berry at regular intervals, but do not cut all the way through. If the berry is large, make 8 cuts.

▪ Using your fingers, gently spread apart the "ruffle" so that it fans out. Then place a sprig of fresh mint with 2 leaves underneath the top of the berry.

EGG YOLK PAINT

Have you always wanted to be an artist? Here is your chance to paint and eat well at the same time. Rolled cookies, piecrusts, and tarts can be decorated with all-natural paints made of egg yolk blended with food paste to produce myriad colors. I recommend professional bakers' food colorings over the supermarket variety (see note on page 110). Paint freehand, or use a stencil as a guide. Buy an assortment of small pastry brushes, but use them only for food, and always wash and dry them thoroughly.

> **For each color of paint, you'll need 1 egg yolk and food paste in colors of your choice.**

▪ In a small bowl, beat a large egg yolk with a drop of the food paste of your choice, adding more color as needed to reach the desired hue. Using a dry, clean brush, paint your design on the cookies, piecrust, or tart, then proceed with baking directions of the food being garnished. For brighter color, bake the food to be garnished first, and within the last 5 minutes of baking time remove the food and brush on the paint. Carefully return the painted food to the oven so as not to disturb the paint, and then finish cooking.

PIECRUST STYLES

*N*ot only are ornamental edgings on pastry crusts beautiful, but they also are practical, as they seal the pastry crusts together for filled pies. A sunburst design is a perfect backdrop for a key lime, coconut custard, lemon meringue, or other tropical pie filling. A rope pattern is a handsome decoration for a pumpkin, mincemeat, or other sophisticated pie. Swiss dot is a great choice to encircle a country-style, fruit-filled pie, such as cherry or blueberry.

You will need the ingredients for your favorite pie.

▪ Line a pie plate with a circle of rolled-out pie dough, following your favorite recipe for dough and using a plate of the dimensions specified. If it is to be filled before baking, line it, fill it, and then top it with a second crust. If the pie is to be filled later, and the crust will be pre-baked, be sure to line it with parchment paper and pie weights (or dried beans) before baking.

▪ Trim the pastry, leaving a 1-inch (2.5-cm) overhang. Tuck the overhang under the dough on the rim of the pie plate to form a thicker edge, while pressing the dough to make an even thickness all the way around.

Making a Sunburst Pattern

■ Press the rounded tip of an inverted spoon along the rim of the pie plate, cutting through the pastry. Reserve the scraps for later use. Repeat all the way around the edge of the crust, at about ⅛-inch (3-mm) intervals, leaving finely pointed triangles in between each cut. Gently cover the edge of the crust with a ring of aluminum foil to prevent it from burning.

■ Follow directions for baking (but omit a glaze), and remove the aluminum foil ring during the last 5 minutes of baking time so that the crust can bake to a light, golden brown, unless it is already browned to desired doneness.

Making a Rope Pattern

■ Roll out 2 ropes of pie dough of equal size and long enough to encircle the pie when joined together. Brush the edge of the crust with lightly beaten egg white, and gently press the 2 ropes onto the crust. Make the ends flush to give the appearance of a continuous ring.

■ Beginning with 1 of the 2 areas where the ropes are attached, use the dull edge of a knife with a thick blade to make diagonal indents into the ropes, pressing down lightly in even increments 1 inch (2.5 cm) apart. Repeat along crust edge.

■ Bake according to directions, brushing the edge of the pie with lightly beaten egg white to glaze. If the crust begins to brown more than desired, cover with aluminum foil.

Making a Swiss-Dot Pattern

■ Press an inverted fork into the edge of a pastry-lined pie plate (using the tines to make a set of four holes). Then press the fork again directly above the first set. You should now have a rectangle of 8 very small holes. Continue this pattern along the edge of the crust to form rows of tiny holes, each set slightly apart.

■ Proceed with the baking, but do not brush with an egg glaze. If the crust begins to brown more than desired, cover with aluminum foil.

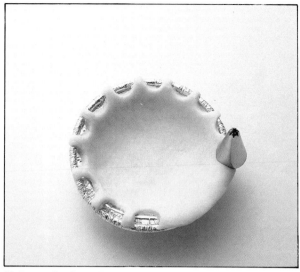

Making a Sunburst Pattern with a pastry tip.

Making a Rope Pattern with the dull edge of a knife.

Making a Swiss-Dot Pattern with a fork.

STAINED-GLASS COOKIES

These cookies will draw an audience every time you bring them to the table. The glittery, translucent centers with a hint of color make a dessert or confection plate shine. Stained-Glass Cookies can be made in any shape or size you want.

> **You will need rolled sugar cookie dough and colored, fruit-flavored hard candies.**

■ Separate the hard candies into groups by color. Place each group into a sturdy, sealed plastic bag. Transfer a bag to your work surface, and with a rolling pin or bottom of a heavy skillet, pound the candies until they are crushed to a very fine powder. Repeat this process with remaining bags of candies and reserve.

■ Follow sugar cookie recipe and, on a lightly floured work surface, roll out dough to a ⅛-inch

(3-mm) thickness. Using cookie cutters, cut out desired shapes, and then cut out the centers of each cookie using a smaller cutter. The centers can also be any shape you want. Or simply echo the pattern of the cookie with a smaller cutter of the same design. For example, a heart-shaped cookie could have a heart-shaped center cutout. Transfer the cookies to an aluminum-foil-lined cookie sheet.

■ Spoon the desired color of crushed candies into the center of each cookie in a smooth, even layer, so that it is ¼ inch (6 mm) deep and no foil is visible.

■ Proceed with baking directions for your cookie recipe until the cookie is done and the center has melted and resembles glass. If the cookies begin to brown more than desired, but they have not yet finished baking, cover the areas lightly with aluminum foil to prevent them from burning on top.

■ Let the cookies stand until cool, and then carefully remove them by gently peeling the aluminum foil from their undersides. This garnish is best made the day of serving. To store, do not refrigerate, but place in an airtight container in a cool, dry place. If the cookies must be stacked to store, separate the layers with waxed paper.

GRILLED FRUIT KEBABS

These ambrosial, fruit-laden batons can be used to highlight plates of sandwiches or as swizzle sticks for summer tropical cocktails and fruit shakes. They look appetizing alongside shallow bowls of ice cream. You can also use them to show off exotic curries and salads. Group a few together, and stick them into a halved watermelon for an edible centerpiece, or serve smaller clusters as a dessert or starter for brunch. Select the length of the bamboo skewer according to how you will display the finished kebabs.

You'll need 1 ripe pineapple and 4 ripe yet firm mangoes to make approximately 20 kebabs, with 2 pieces of fruit each, depending on the size of the original fruit. Cut the fruit when it is at room temperature to prevent it from splitting upon being skewered.

▪ Peel and core the pineapple. Peel the mangoes, and slice off the 2 fleshy cheeks from each, cutting as close to the large pit as possible. Cut the pineapple crosswise into $^1\!/_3$-inch- (8-mm-) thick rings, and then cut each ring into pointed triangles of equal size. Cut the mango cheeks crosswise into $^1\!/_3$-inch- (8-mm-) slices, and then cut each slice into several blunt triangles (one with the top point cut off). Lay all the fruit sections flat on an aluminum-foil-lined, heat-proof work surface—a metal cookie sheet works well.

Mango and pineapple slices.

Place the hot metal skewer tip diagonally across the mango slice.

■ Wearing long, flameproof mitts, place the first 3 inches (8 cm) (starting at the point) of a long, metal, flat, or round skewer on a stove burner directly on the heat source. (Bamboo skewers will be used for displaying the garnish.) *Be very careful—do not leave the skewer unattended.* Let the skewer stand in the heat for 2 minutes. Wearing your mitts, transfer the skewer (holding the cool handle) to the fruit triangles. Place the hot skewer tip onto a pineapple triangle, and hold it there for 30 seconds. When you lift it off there should be a light brown "grill" mark. If the mark is too dark for your taste, leave the next skewer on for less time; if the mark is too light, leave it on longer.

■ Return the skewer to the heat for 2 minutes, and then repeat, making a second mark on the pineapple, dividing it into thirds. Return the skewer to the heat for 2 more minutes, and then place the tip diagonally across the mango triangle. Repeat the process as with the pineapple, but make 3 marks on the diagonal, dividing the mango triangle into quarters. Repeat until all the pieces have markings.

■ Gently push a bamboo skewer, pointed end first, through the center of the bottom end of a blunt mango triangle. Push it in straight so it does not go through the back, but through the center of the top edge of the slice. Then push the skewer up through the center of the top edge of a pineapple triangle. Repeat with the remaining fruit slices and bamboo skewers.

Creating Variations

■ You can create other kebabs using a variety of fruits. Always use fruit in season that will exhibit the grill marks well. For example, 2 deep reddish black Bing cherries flanking a single pale yellowish pink Royal Ann cherry, looks beautiful when grilled. (Leave the stems on for extra visual appeal, being careful not to burn them when making the grill marks.) Or try combining 4 red raspberries and 4 golden raspberries, in an alternating pattern.

CANDY SUSHI

*A*dd *a splash of color to your next dessert with Candy Sushi. These fancy spirals mimic the ever-popular Japanese sushi, but are made with candied fruit. They are particularly fun topping a parfait, custard, or pudding. Pass them at the end of a meal in place of fresh fruit, or display them in a candy tray. Dried apricot paste is the main ingredient for this garnish, and it is available at Middle Eastern grocery stores. Or buy pressed dried fruits (also referred to as "chewy fruit snacks" or "leathers"), available in many flavors and colors, at your supermarket in the cookie or candy section. Unusual dried fruits—such as blueberries, cranberries, and cherries—are now available through mail-order sources.*

> For 8 to 10 garnishes, you'll need 8½ ounces (238 g) dried apricot paste, 2 ounces (56 g) sweetened, flaked coconut, and 1 ounce (28 g) dried fruits.

▪ Lay a rectangular-shaped piece of dried apricot paste, shiny side down, on a sheet of waxed paper.

▪ Spread a thin layer of sweetened, flaked coconut on the apricot paste, so no apricot paste shows through. Pack down the coconut by pressing firmly with your palms.

▪ Scatter a colorful assortment of small, pitted, dried fruit on top of the coconut. The fruits pictured here are seedless golden raisins, dried blueberries, and dried cranberries.

▪ Starting with the short end, slowly roll up the "sushi" tightly, pressing down on the fruit and coconut as you roll to make sure that there are no bald spots. Wrap the roll tightly in two layers of plastic wrap, and store at room temperature for up to 2 weeks.

▪ When ready to serve, unwrap the sushi and place it on a cutting board, seam side down. Using a serrated knife, cut the sushi crosswise, into ½-inch- (2-cm-) thick slices, slicing only what you need, and rewrapping the remainder so it won't dry out. Press the surface of the filling of sushi with your fingers to tighten any wisps of coconut or loose fruit and serve.

WHOLE ALMOND BARK

*J*ewellike praline—an almond-and-sugar confection—is a lovely and versatile garnish. For this garnish, it can be broken into shards of almond bark, ground in a food processor until it becomes a glimmering powder, or simply used to coat individual toasted almonds to make small, elegant, oval-shaped garnishes. The almonds are toasted first to bring out their flavor.

Use pieces of almond bark or ground powder to decorate ice cream, cakes, poached fruit, custards, or any dessert. The Individual Caramel-Coated Almonds work well for savory cuisine, such as rice, seafood, or chicken dishes—and sweet dishes, including parfaits, candies, and cupcakes.

> **You will need 2¼ ounces (6 g) whole (unblanched) almonds, ½ teaspoon (3 ml) lemon juice, ½ cup (112 g) granulated sugar, and 2 tablespoons (30 ml) water.**

■ Preheat oven to 350 degrees F (175 degrees C). Spread the almonds on a shallow baking pan, and bake for 10 to 12 minutes, or until lightly golden. Turn them once after 5 minutes. Transfer immediately to a wire rack to prevent them from becoming burned. Set aside until ready to use.

■ Lightly grease an aluminum-foil-lined shallow baking pan. Arrange a single layer of toasted almonds so they are touching one another. You can arrange them into a design, such as a flower or a sun, or just scatter them. If making individual Caramel-Coated Almonds, set aside however many you need.

■ In a medium saucepan over low heat, combine the lemon juice, sugar, and water. Cook until the sugar has dissolved and the liquid is clear (about 2 to 4 minutes), stirring often. (Be careful—wear flameproof mitts and avoid sugar burns.)

Ingredients for the Almond Bark.

Pour the caramel mixture over the almonds until well coated.

▪ Raise the heat to medium, and bring to a boil. Boil without stirring until the mixture is golden (about 10 to 15 minutes) and reaches the hard-crack stage (300 degrees F, or 150 degrees C) on a candy thermometer, or until a small piece of the mixture solidifies immediately when dropped into a bowl of cold water.

To Make Almond Bark

▪ Pour all of the caramel mixture over the layer of almonds until well coated. Let stand at room temperature until hard. Peel the aluminum foil from the back until the bark is released from the foil. Break into pieces, or grind the bark in a food processor until it forms a powder.

Making Individual Caramel-Coated Almonds

▪ Reserve about a teaspoon (5 ml) of the caramel in the pan for every individual almond to be coated. Then stir in the reserved almonds until well coated. Lift each almond out with a slotted spoon, letting the excess caramel drip off. Immediately transfer to a corner of the prepared baking sheet used for making almond bark. Repeat with the remaining almonds, placing the almonds about 2 inches (5 cm) apart.

▪ Let stand until the coating is firm, then peel the foil from the back of the almonds until they are released. Break off any excess caramel from the sides of the individual almonds. This garnish is best made the day of serving. To store, package in an airtight container, and store in a cool, dry place. Do not refrigerate.

Note: Here are some tips for working with caramel:

Do not try to make caramel in humid weather, as it will not harden completely and will be sticky.

Use a pan that conducts heat evenly and quickly, such as copper (not tin because the melting point of tin is below that of caramel) or Calphalon,™ so that the cooking stops soon after the pan is removed from the heat.

To prevent cracking a thermometer used for caramel, let the thermometer cool completely before rinsing.

For easy clean up, soak the pan used for caramel in hot water to help dissolve and remove the candy.

FLOWER FANTASY

The following is a list of some of the most common edible flowers, which make perfect ingredients for garnishes. Edible flowers come in a variety of shapes, colors, and flavors. Always check more than 1 reliable source as to whether a flower is edible, and make sure it has been grown organically (pesticide-free). Use only the flower blossoms or petals from the following list, not the leaves or stems, unless it is a commonly known edible culinary herb, such as dill, basil, or chives, or this list specifies that the leaves are edible, as with nasturtiums. For some flowers, 2 or more of their common names are listed.

ANISE HYSSOP FLOWERS
ARUGULA FLOWERS
BASIL FLOWERS, SWEET
BEAN BLOSSOMS, PAINTED LADY
BORAGE
CALENDULA
CARNATION
CHAMOMILE
CHERVIL FLOWERS
CHIVE FLOWERS
CLOVER, RED
CORNFLOWER, BACHELOR'S BUTTON
DAISY (*Bellis perennis,* from the *Compositae* family.
     Do *not* eat the American equivalent.)
DANDELION
DAYLILY
DILL FLOWERS

HEARTSEASE, JOHNNY-JUMP-UPS
    (eat only in small amounts,
    a tablespoon [15 ml] or less)
HONEYSUCKLE
LAVENDER
MARIGOLDS, LEMON
MINT FLOWERS
MUSTARD, FIELD
NASTURTIUM FLOWERS AND LEAVES
PANSIES
    (eat only in small amounts,
    a tablespoon [15 ml] or less)
ROSE PETALS
ROSEMARY FLOWERS
SAGE FLOWERS
SNAPDRAGONS
SQUASH BLOSSOMS
THYME FLOWERS
VIOLETS, SWEET

MAIL-ORDER SOURCES

AMERICAN SPOON FOODS
411 East Lake Street
Petoskey, MI 49770
(616) 347-9030

Products include a wide assortment of nuts and delicious and unusual dried fruits, such as blueberries, cranberries, and sour cherries. Catalog available.

BALDUCCI'S
424 Avenue of the Americas
New York, NY 10011
(212) 673-2600

Mail-Order Division:
In New York State:
(800) 247-2450
Outside of New York State:
(800) 822-1444

Many specialty foods available, including a large variety of fresh pasta, fresh herbs, smoked salmon, and caviar. Catalog available.

BRIDGE KITCHENWARE
214 East 52nd Street
New York, NY 10022
(212) 688-4220

Wide assortment of cookware, including some very specialized tools; large selection of pastry equipment. Catalog available.

BROADWAY PANHANDLER
520 Broadway
New York, NY 10012
(212) 966-3434

Bakeware, cookware, and household goods. A fun place to visit and browse.

THE CHOCOLATE GALLERY
34 West 22nd Street
New York, NY 10010
(212) 675-CAKE

Dependable resource for cake-decorating equipment, candy supplies, handmade frosting decorations, cookie cutters, and unusual items such as edible gold leafs, and gold and silver powders. Classes offered. Catalog available.

DAISY HYDRO FARMS
P.O. Box 600
Southhold, NY 11971
(516) 765-5181

This farm supplies beautiful edible flowers to well-known restaurants and stores. Call for product information.

DEAN & DELUCA
560 Broadway
New York, NY 10012
(212) 431-1691

Mail-Order Division:
Outside of New York State:
(800) 221-7714

Very large selection of gourmet goods, including saffron, bridge-theme sugar cubes (hearts, diamonds, clubs, and spades), preserved sun-dried tomatoes, and many other exotic foods. Fabulous selection of dried pasta, grains, and beans. They also sell kitchen utensils. Catalog available.

FOWLER'S GOURMET
Brightleaf Square
905 West Main Street
Durham, NC 27701
(919) 683-2555

*Carries fancy baking supplies and garnishes,
such as crystalized roses, violets, mint leaves,
and ginger. Other items include almond paste,
glacéed fruits, and a large variety of chocolate.
Catalog available.*

**FRIEDA'S FINEST/PRODUCE
SPECIALTIES, INC.**
P.O. Box 58488
Los Angeles, CA 90058
(213) 627-2981

*Carries a large inventory of hard-to-find
vegetables, including cactus pads and pousse-
pied, as well as international fruits. Also carries
fresh Chinese noodles, fresh herbs, dried fruits—
including dried persimmons and crystalized
ginger—and ornamentals, such as strawberry
corn. Call for product information.*

KITCHENIQUE
872 Highway 98 East
Destin, FL 32541
(904) 837-1183

*Mail-Order Division:
Outside of Florida State:*
(800) 476-2918

*French candy seashells, and chocolate-covered
espresso beans. Catalog available.*

MAID OF SCANDINAVIA
3244 Raleigh Avenue
Minneapolis, MN 55416
(612) 927-7996

*Mail-Order Division:
Outside of Minnesota State:*
(800) 328-6722

*Immense stock of specialized baking ingredients.
Also carries candy-making equipment, molds,
and a large supply of doilies and wrappings.
Source for marzipan and professional food pastes.*

PASQUALE BROTHERS DOWNTOWN LTD.
217 King Street East
Toronto, Ontario
M58 1J9
(416) 364-7397

*Wholesalers to top restaurants. Also provide
retail gourmet groceries.*

PRICE AE FINE FOODS LTD.
181 Bank Street
Ottawa, Ontario
K2P 1W5
(613) 232-3557

*Fresh meat, produce, herbs, and fancy groceries
can be found here.*

SAFFRON'S
Manotick Mews Shopping Centre
Box #208
Manotick, Ontario
K0A 290
(613) 692-2064

*A purveyor of fine foods, including exotic items,
such as saffron.*

VAN REX GOURMET FOODS, INC.
120 Imlay Street
Brooklyn, NY 11231
(718) 858-8887

A large variety of baking chocolate, including Prestige, Suchard/Tobler, and Valrhona. Catalog available.

WILLIAMS–SONOMA
Mail-Order Department
P.O. Box 7456
San Francisco, CA 94120-7456
(415) 421-4242

Great selection of well-made cooking and baking tools. Catalog available.

WORLDWIDE IMPORTED FOODS, INC.
6700 Côte des Neiges
Montreal, Quebec
H3S 2B2
(514) 733-1463

International gourmet foods and cookware.

TEMPLATES

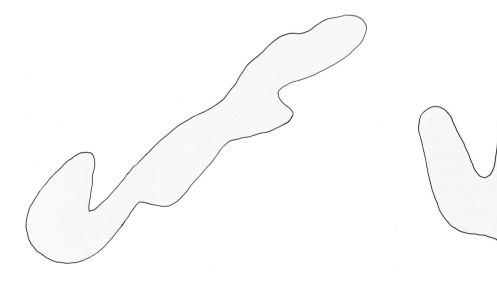

Tex-Mex Tortillas

Polenta Basket

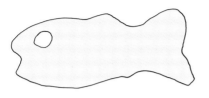
Tricolor Bell Pepper Fish

For cooking and baking convenience, we suggest that you use the following table for adapting to metric measurement. The table gives approximate, rather than exact, conversions.

Spoons

¼ teaspoon	=	1 milliliter
½ teaspoon	=	2 milliliters
1 teaspooon	=	5 milliliters
1 tablespoon	=	15 milliliters
2 tablespoons	=	25 milliliters
3 tablespoons	=	50 milliliters

Cups

¼ cup	=	50 milliliters
⅓ cup	=	75 milliliters
½ cup	=	125 milliliters
⅔ cup	=	150 milliliters
¾ cup	=	175 milliliters
1 cup	=	250 milliliters
1 pint	=	500 milliliters
1 quart	=	.95 liters
1 gallon	=	3.8 liters

Oven Temperatures

200°F	=	100°C
225°F	=	110°C
250°F	=	120°C
275°F	=	140°C
300°F	=	150°C
325°F	=	160°C
350°F	=	180°C
375°F	=	190°C
400°F	=	200°C
425°F	=	220°C
450°F	=	230°C
475°F	=	240°C

To Adapt Lengths

one inch	=	2.5 centimeters
one foot	=	30 centimeters
one yard	=	.9 meters

To Adapt Weights

one ounce	=	28 grams
one pound	=	.45 kilograms

INDEX